✸ Man of Aztlan ✸

Man of Aztlan

A Biography of Rudolfo Anaya

Abelardo Baeza, Ph.D.

EAKIN PRESS   Austin, Texas

This book is dedicated to my brothers and sisters:
Tomas
Frances (Panchita)
Maria
Armando
and to Lily,
who went to Heaven in 1992
and is in my heart always.

All photographs are printed courtesy of
Rudolfo and Patricia Anaya.

For CIP information,
please access:
www.loc.gov

FIRST EDITION
Copyright © 2001
By Abelardo Baeza
Published in the U.S.A.
By Eakin Press
A Division of Sunbelt Media, Inc.
P.O. Drawer 90159
Austin, Texas 78709-0159
email: eakinpub@sig.net
website: www.eakinpress.com
ALL RIGHTS RESERVED.
1   2   3   4   5   6   7   8   9
1-57168-564-2

Contents

A Poem for Anaya

If I could not tell what I have come to know,
what would my life have been:
my soul would have ceased to grow.
For the writer must pen—
record,
set down in print
the truths in his word
his spirit and grace,
La Raza, Aztlán,
yet Americán;
his place and stint
in time,
what he has lived
or can imagine—
equally valid,
equally sublime.

N. C. Sager
June 1999

January 22, 2001

Dear Dr. Baeza,

I am writing to offer my congratulations to you on the completion of your biography of my husband Rudolfo. You have set a precedent for the completion of a biography of a Chicano author. The manuscript is timely, and will certainly be of interest and an aid to young readers doing research on Rudolfo's background and writing. The chronology of his life will be most helpful to anyone interested in the development of the life of a writer. I was pleased with your summary of his books. The writing was succinct yet gave the flavor of each work.

You have captured his role as a leader in the Chicano movement. As you have stated, I too, believe Rudy appeared on the scene at the right time to leave his mark in the history of American literature as an innovator and recorder of Chicano literature. His first novel BLESS ME ULTIMA set the tone and paved the pathway for many fine publications by Chicano/a writers.

Rudy is a dedicated man to his work and his love for his people. He committed himself to record the history and traditions of the Mexican-American Chicano culture for the young people who might forget what has come before.

In addition to his dedication has been his generosity in giving his time and energy to his writing and teaching. Through his creative writing classes he has helped many young writers to a successful career in writing. He has also established scholarships to aid needy students.

Again, thank you for your dedication in bringing this biography to completion.

Most sincerely,
Patricia Anaya

Acknowledgments

I am grateful to these great individuals at Sul Ross State University who were very helpful and supportive as I researched and wrote Rudolfo Anaya's biography:

Dr. David Cockrum, vice president for academic affairs, "Uncle Dave," who has been a witness to my work and a loyal friend over the years;

Dr. Felipe de Ortego y Gasca, professor of English and education, my "*Padrino*" who offered solid advice and constructive criticism about the manuscript;

Dr. Nelson C. Sager, professor of English, a talented man and good friend, who read my work and shared his ideas and views;

Dr. Jim Case, professor of political science, good friend and brother, who has always offered his help and understanding;

Leo and Elsa Dominguez, my *compadres*, whose friendship and bond in God I cherish;

Baldemar and Araceli Garza, good friends and former students who have always kept in touch and of whom I am profoundly proud;

Paul Olsen, director of the print shop, who has always assisted me when I call on him;

Cathie Hope, fantastic secretary and friend, who helped me so much with the preparation of the manuscript.

Special thanks to:

Rudolfo and Patricia Anaya, good friends and mentors, whose words of encouragement through letters, phone calls, and conversations have provided the incentives needed to complete the biography. Through them, *Man of Aztlan* has become a dream come true.

—Photo by Marion Ettlinger

Introduction:
The Man Behind the Stories

"Ultima came to stay with us the summer I was almost seven. When she came the beauty of the *llano* unfolded before my eyes, and the gurgling waters of the river sang to the hum of the turning earth. The magical time of childhood stood still, and the pulse of the living earth pressed its mystery into my living blood. She took my hand, and the silent, magic powers she possessed made beauty from the raw, sun-baked *llano,* the green river valley, and the blue bowl which was the white sun's home. My bare feet felt the throbbing earth and my body trembled with excitement. Time stood still, and it shared with me all that had been, and all that was to come..." (*Bless Me, Ultima,* p. 1)

Young readers are assigned to read *Bless Me, Ultima, Heart of Aztlan,* or *Tortuga* by Rudolfo Anaya in their Multicultural Studies classes. Children in the elementary grades read *The Farolitos of Christmas* and *Farolitos for Abuelo* during the holiday season. Junior historians hear *The Legend of La Llorona* and *Billy the Kid* during the folklore and folktale festival. Aspiring actors peruse *Matachines, Angie,* or *Who Killed Don Jose?* in their search for the right scene to present for play competition. Travel enthusiasts read *A Chicano in China* and notice the parallels between two diverse cultures.

As students, they know the familiar way of previewing and selecting fiction and non-fiction books for oral reports and term papers. When they examine books, they notice the length and the cover design. Examining a copy of *Bless Me, Ultima,* Anaya's first novel, they see an interesting cover that features the figures of an old woman, a young boy, and an owl drawn on a black background.

When reading the opening paragraph, students hear Anaya's voice in luminous prose. He presents his characters in a realistic portrait of life in a small town in New Mexico during World War II. From the arrival of "La Grande" in the Marez home to the heart-wrenching ending, readers follow the sequence of events narrated in Anaya's lyrical style. Ultima reminds them of their mothers, grandmothers, or *madrinas.* Tony's narration is penetrating and nostalgic as he recalls the presence of Ultima in the Marez household.

In preparation for the critical essay or book report on *Ultima,* young scholars seek information in the library or on the Internet about Anaya and his works, which are now part of public school and university curricula. They read excerpts from his novels, short stories, plays, children's books, and essays, and find reviews for their papers in periodicals and journals.

As students are given lists of "highly recommended" books, they spot Anaya's novel. Published in 1972 by Quinto Sol Publications, *Bless Me, Ultima* is used by teachers of English, Bilingual Education, and ESL classes as a bridge over which readers walk into the world of Chicano Literature. They discover that the novel is the first of a trilogy that includes *Heart of Aztlan* and *Tortuga*. Anaya's novels give readers an insight into the life of Chicanos in the Southwest.

Bless Me, Ultima has become the most recognized Chicano novel of all time. It is more than the story of a boy growing up in Guadalupe, New Mexico, in the 1940s. Rudolfo Anaya creates a tapestry of realistic characters, scenes, and actions. Students find the book enticing because the story is narrated by the young hero, Tony Marez, a boy almost seven years old at the beginning of the story. He is a child with an awesome capacity for learning. He dreams of the people in the family home on the night that his mother, Maria, brings him into the world. Tony dreams about his brothers, León, Eugene, and Andrew, who are soldiers in Europe. Deborah and Theresa, his sisters, stir his curiosity about *la curandera,* or faith healer, named Ultima as he listens to them talk about her being called a *bruja,* or witch. This will not be the only time that Tony will hear this whispered about Ultima.

When Ultima arrives to live with the family, Tony is immediately drawn to the old woman and her knowledge of life. She introduces him to the wonders of medicinal herbs found in the countryside and used to cure people of everything from *mal de ojo* (the evil eye) to *mal de susto* (fright). Ultima comforts him when he is frightened by the death of Lupito, the town's misunderstood military veteran.

Her understanding of people and their behavior is mesmerizing to Tony. In essence, Ultima becomes a shaman who helps Tony and others who seek her advice.

During the course of the novel, Tony witnesses several events around Guadalupe that affect his life. He becomes part of a circle of friends and enjoys the camaraderie of the boys with whom he associates. The boy will live through an incredible seventh year of his life. In a time span of twelve months, Tony's journey from innocent child to impressionable prepubescent unfolds. He learns intriguing facts about his family, culture, history, and folklore—and even more about life and death.

Many young readers comment that they can identify with the characters because members of the gang—Horse, Cico, Samuel, Abel, the Vitamin Kid, and Jasón—talk and act like kids they know. These boys laugh, fight, play, and learn about life. Some, like Tony Marez, learn to read and write in English for the first time, while others, like Florence, face tragedies within their families. These young boys are sons of people who struggle to survive in Guadalupe as World War II smolders on foreign soil.

Adolescents are introduced to the world of Tony Marez. His spirit soars above Guadalupe in the same manner that Ultima's owl flies over her as she continues her journey of healing. In *Shaman of Words,* one of Anaya's essays, the opening lines present the prophecy of Tony's birth: "An owl calls from a juniper tree ... I am to arrive at one of the adobe homes tonight ... This is how it begins ... A woman in labor" (p. 1). This essay and Anaya's

Autobiography, written in 1985, are excellent primary sources that readers will want to consult as they experience the novel. They will develop a better understanding of Anaya's use of stream-of-consciousness and the relevance of Tony's dreams.

As Tony matures, he has dream visions of the tragic events that will occur. He sees the ghost of Lupito after the disturbed man dies at the hands of an angry posse. Likewise, he has dreams of Narciso, the town drunk, who is killed by Tenorio Trementina in a snow storm, and Florence, the little *güerito* (little blond boy) who drowns in Blue Lake. In truth, these dreams represent Tony's subconscious—a place where he keeps his ideas, fears, doubts, and questions about life, death, and mortality. Anaya presents the physical and spiritual facets of the boy's life in living color.

As readers continue to study the novel, they will have questions about the characters and plot. Will Tenorio carry out his plan to destroy Ultima? Will he cause harm to Tony? Will Tony and Ultima survive? Will Tony grow up and become a priest? Is Ultima a witch?

The quest to find answers to these questions makes the novel a unique reading experience. The plot intensifies and the series of actions leading to the climax of the story inspire students to continue reading and taking notes. They want to know what is going to happen to Uncle Lucas, Florence, the Trementina sisters, Tenorio, Ultima, and Tony. Scenes such as Ultima's "test" to prove her innocence at the hands of an angry mob and Tony's blessing of Narciso in a blinding snowstorm make the novel impossible to leave in the locker after class.

There are many elements of the book that young readers must examine—plot, characters, symbolism, irony, style of narration, and effect. And they learn to savor a realistic story set in the Southwest. Anaya's descriptions of the *llano,* or plains, are breath-taking. The legend of the Golden Carp is a beautiful story the author created. And that day at Blue Lake when Florence dives into the water and fails to surface is a tragic and suspenseful scene.

Many questions surface from young readers as they continue to read. Why does Florence return to the waters ruled by the mysterious gold fish? Is he the reincarnation of the Aztec Prince? Will Ultima live to see Tenorio pay for his crimes? Where did Anaya find the inspiration for writing the novel? What is the significance of the owl in the novel?

It is my hope that as people read *Man of Aztlan,* they will find answers to these questions and understand Rudolfo Anaya's role in Chicano Literature. Readers will see the genesis of *Bless Me, Ultima,* a novel which took almost seven years to write, and the works that have followed. The study also contains pertinent information about the literature which grew out of the Chicano Movement in the 1960s and has evolved into an integral part of American Literature.

Man of Aztlan presents Rudolfo Anaya's story from his birth to his present-day life. Readers will see him as a boy with a tremendous imagination who evolves into an intelligent, ambitious young man who aspires to be a writer. His college years and the start of a career in academia are also examined. The publication of Anaya's first novel marks a turning point in his life. From there, he is seen traveling around the country, promoting *Bless Me, Ultima,* and writing the novels, short stories, plays, and children's books that have made him the most famous Chicano writer of our time.

It is my sincere hope that *Man of Aztlan* will accomplish its goal—to portray accurately and truthfully the life of the man who is regarded as the "Godfather of the Chicano Literary Movement." Readers will discover his penchant as master storyteller and hear his voice in the novels, short stories, dramas, historical fiction, and children's books that have captured international attention. Because he lives in New Mexico, his stories have become important components of Southwestern Literature. Anaya opens the door to a world of mystery and adventure, two themes popular in adolescent fiction.

I am honored to have the opportunity to relate the story of this talented author. There are many studies written about Rudolfo Anaya. As students research materials for term projects, panel presentations, critical essays, they will find character sketches in *The Dictionary of Literary Biography,* newspaper and magazine articles, and literary reviews. Book jackets contain pictures and biographical data. Books such as *Chicano Authors,* edited by Juan Bruce-Novoa, and *Conversations With Rudolfo Anaya,* edited by Bruce Dick and Silvio Sirias, have biographical pieces and chronologies of his life and works. Anaya's 1986 autobiography, published by Gale Research Company, is very helpful; yet there are no biographies of him for young adults.

Likewise, I have compiled a file of articles, reviews, pictures, and autographed first editions of all his works. I always hoped that these materials would evolve into a full-length book based on Anaya's life. My collection is presently found in a walnut box in my office, complete with its own computerized card catalogue. It was begun by my graduate student, Mary L. Dutchover of Fort Davis, Texas, in the first Rudolfo Anaya Seminar taught in 1993.

I have been teaching Chicano Literature for almost two decades and have given lectures to primary, middle school, and high school students on Chicano novels, folktales, plays, and children's books. Middle school and high school readers working on term papers on these topics look for Rudolfo Anaya and his literature. They often request interviews and copies of articles.

When I address educators attending conferences and symposia focusing on multicultural literary studies, I am always asked a familiar question—when will a biography of Anaya be written? That time has arrived, and it is my pleasure to present *Man of Aztlan*. Readers will see the many facets of his life as writer, scholar, historian, world traveler, and husband to his wife, Patricia. In essence, they will know the creator of *Bless Me, Ultima,* the novel that defines the true essence of Chicano Literature. At last, they will meet the man behind the stories.

ABELARDO BAEZA, PH.D.

Chapter 1

A Child Reaches for a Pencil

"This is Pastura, New Mexico. The year is 1937. I am to arrive at one of the adobe homes tonight."

(Shaman of Words, p.1)

Rudolfo Anaya shares many common traits with Tony in *Bless Me, Ultima.* In the novel, the youngest child of Gabriel and Maria Marez is brought into this world by Ultima, the *curandera,* who was the midwife at the births of his brothers and sisters. As is customary, the men sit outside, talk, smoke, and drink. When the first cries of life are heard, they toast to the birth and present gifts to the baby boy.

Among the presents is a saddle from his father, a symbol of the *llaneros,* the *vaqueros* of the plains. A neighbor brings a horse blanket. Others bring bottles of whiskey, a new rope, a bridle, chaps, and a new guitar.

Rudolfo Anaya had a similar birth. He was welcomed by the *vecinos,* or neighbors, and friends of the family. He was told by his mother, Rafaelita, about an interesting event that occurred as he was beginning to crawl. The fam-

1

ily members gathered around, and each person placed different objects around the baby. Martin Anaya, his father, put a saddle in front of his son because he wanted him to be a *vaquero* (cowboy). Someone placed paper and a pencil. His mother said, "Perhaps it was me, because I had always yearned for an education.... Anyway, you crawled to the paper and pencil" (Anaya, *Autobiography*, p.4).

His mother, Rafaelita, is the daughter of Liborio Mares, a farmer from the Puerto de Luna on the Pecos River. She is the daughter of farmers who raise families and grow crops. Furthermore, they tend to their sheep, pigs, and cows.

Rafaelita left the valley to marry a *vaquero* who preferred to ride horses and work cattle. His name was Salomon Bonney. She bore a son and a daughter. Her husband died a few years after their marriage. Says Anaya, "a frightened horse that rears and throws its rider can kill even the best *vaquero*."

The young widow then married Martin Anaya, a man who worked as a ranch hand. He knew how to work cattle and sheep. From this union came seven children—Larry, Martin, Edwina, Angelina, Rudolfo, Dolores, and Loretta. Martin Anaya had been married before and had a daughter from that union. "Later I will know her as a sister," states Anaya. "I know nothing about the first woman in my father's life."

Rudolfo Alfonso Anaya was born on 30 October 1937, in Pastura, a small town south of Santa Rosa in eastern New Mexico. His mother told him that he came into the world with the umbilical cord tied around his neck. In *Shaman of*

Anaya's birth home, photographed in 1999.

Words, he asks prophetic questions, similar to those asked by Tony Marez to Ultima: "Was I born a hanged man? Was I close to death at my birth? Or did I not want to leave the womb?"

He was reared in Santa Rosa, a small farming and ranching community. He was under the impression that the entire world spoke Spanish. "It was a struggle to learn English at school," he says, "but learn I did. . . . Later, I was to include many of the experiences of those years into my first novel."

As a small boy, he recalls playing with his sisters and eating hot tortillas with butter. Sitting in the kitchen with his mother, he would ask many questions about the current of life. The Chavez boys were his neighbors and best friends. They played hide-and-go-seek, tag, and football.

Many hours were spent swimming in the Pecos River and sitting around campfires at night, telling stories and arguing like typical boys. They had fights with the town boys, and Anaya remembers accidentally shooting Santiago Chavez in the eye with a BB gun. This is a frightening incident that haunted him for a long time.

He ran around barefooted and wore shoes only for Sunday church or to the movies in town on Saturday. With his dog, Sporty, by his side, he was not afraid of anything around him. A child with a vivid imagination, Rudolfo hated to travel alone along the river. He had been told that *la Llorona,* the fabled mother who had killed her own child, was hiding in the dense brushes along the bank. When he had to cut wild alfalfa to feed his rabbits, he found himself alone—in a world full of strange powers.

His mother wanted him to be a priest, but his father, like Gabriel Marez in *Bless Me, Ultima,* secretly disliked the idea. Martin Anaya had been a *vaquero* who had traded his life in the *llano* for a more domestic one in town. Rafelita told Rudolfo many folktales which opened his imagination and developed an interest in literature.

His love of books started early in life. Anaya recalls his days in the small library in Santa Rosa in an interview conducted by John F. Crawford (*Conversations With Rudolfo Anaya*). He says, "I would visit it periodically, starting at an early age, when I was in grade school. It was a little one-room library actually placed on top of the fire house on the first floor, where there was an old beaten up fire truck used on a volunteer basis when there was a fire in the town. We

4

Rudolfo Anaya's third-grade class at Santa Rosa, New Mexico. "Rudy" is third from right, bottom row.

climbed up the rickety steps to the little room that was the library. That interests me too, you know, looking back at what was formative in my love of books" (p. 105).

Anaya remembers an aunt who came to live with the Marez family and died of cancer. He had grown very close to her. Martin Anaya made a coffin from pine planks, and the *velorio,* or wake, was held in the family parlor. Coins were placed on his aunt's eyes to keep them closed. After the rosary was said, Rudolfo and a little girl were awarded the coins.

In *Bless Me, Ultima,* Tony Marez has a difficult time learning the magic of the letters from Miss Maestas, his first-grade teacher. But he does. At the end of the first day of school, Tony goes home and shows his mother his *primeras letras,* his first letters.

Rudolfo Anaya's fascination with the magic of the letters was almost the same. School was not difficult for him because he was learning things in a different way from most children who lived in town. He experienced the elements of nature unfamiliar to the town kids. He saw the nighthawks flying over the desolate *llano* and felt the chill of the wind as he walked home. These images of the *llano* and the lakes around Santa Rosa helped him to develop his creativity and a deep interest in writing.

Anaya remembers his friend, George Gonzalez, whose father had been a sheriff before being tragically killed. George had to step into his father's place and run the ranch. Rudolfo helped him with his chores and remembers the ranch as being a terribly lonely and deserted place.

He attended school in Santa Rosa until eighth grade. In his autobiography, Anaya recalls the disintegration of the gang of boys with whom he played. He observed the separation of people into two main groups—Mexican and Anglo. Prior to that time, he was aware of his Mexican roots and cultural pride, but it was during his elementary school years that he became aware of racial prejudice in the small town where he lived until he was fourteen years old. Like the Chavez family in *Heart of Aztlan,* Martin and Rafaelita decided to move to Albuquerque in search of a better life for themselves and their children.

As a teenager, Rudolfo attended Washington Junior High School and Albuquerque High School. He played baseball, basketball, and rode bikes. His was a typical teenager's life. And then tragedy struck when he was sixteen.

While swimming in an irrigation ditch, he dove into the water and fractured his neck. He floated in the water, unable to move. "I lived through the near-death experience. I saw my soul rising in the air, looking back on a reality I was leaving." He describes the days that followed as being "a horror." He was running a high fever and was strapped to a pulley that went around his chin. Weights were used to hold his neck straight.

When that treatment did not work, a doctor bore holes into his skull and placed pins to hold the ropes of the pulley that were attached to the headboard. Says Anaya, "The 'Rudy' of my childhood was dead—died in nights of tortured fever while he hung on ropes." After he was taken down from the ropes and the pulley, he was driven to a hospital in the middle of the southern New Mexico desert. "My stay in the hospital was my *jornada del muerto*, my journey of the dead. I had died."

In the hospital, Rudolfo Anaya was placed in a body cast. "I became a turtle," he writes in *Shaman of Words*. His family came to visit and pray for his recovery. He was trained to deal with his pain and suffering by those who could move around. Depressed about his traumatic experience, he withdrew into his shell. His nights were filled with nightmares. Voices which had haunted him before were around him. He has described the amazing transformation that took place in the hospital as the wounded youth attempted to question the purpose of his existence. He escaped from the horrors of reality into the world of the soul.

Anaya struggled to feed himself and escape from the cast. He was evolving into a new person, but yearned to be the old one. After a long stay in the hospital, he was released and recalls being "skinny as a board." At home, he was greeted by family and friends. When he was able to walk around the neighborhood, he found a boy who had been in the hospital at the same time. They bonded—just like Tony Marez did in *Bless Me, Ultima* with George and Willy, the outcasts from the farms around Delia, who have to eat their lunches outside Miss Maesta's classroom because they are different from the other children. Anaya identifies with them when he says in *Shaman of Words*, "I don't want to be different!"

The healing process was slow. Anaya's mother helped. Rafaelita massaged life back into her son's body. During this time, he was losing his faith in the church. He struggled with loneliness. He called it "a struggle of human bondage."

In time, he became stronger and began to live a normal life. Friends and classmates were a part of his life once more. On the outside, Rudolfo Anaya was nothing more than a skinny boy. But inside, he had visions of the spiritual side of people.

After a summer at Carrie Tingley Hospital, he returned home and walked with a cane. One of the first things he did was to go to the YMCA—alone. Waiting until everyone was gone, Rudolfo stepped to the edge of the pool. His muscles were weak and stiff. He dove into the water, floated to the top, smiled, dog-paddled out, and sat on the side of the pool. He had conquered one fear within. The healing process had begun.

In the months that followed, he protected those fears and doubts within himself. "I learned the true meaning of loneliness... how if feels to be alone," he writes in his autobiography (p. 11). He had the support of his family and friends. His mother nursed him through the worst part of the paralysis. He was alone and wondering how something so horrible could have happened to him.

Chapter 2

Dudes, Ducktails, and James Dean

"The fifties, as we are being told by the historians of popular culture, were a great time. They were."

(*Autobiography,* p. 12)

The Anaya family moved to Albuquerque in 1952. Martin and Rafaelita's house was in the Barelas *barrio,* at 433 Pacific. Rudolfo's brother, Larry, lived in Barelas and knew the area and the people, so Rudolfo had no problems in adapting to his new environment. Many Mexican American people were moving from the small towns into cities like Albuquerque in search of work. The streets soon became crowded with gangs of *pachucos.*

For spending money, Rudolfo and his friend Robert Martinez cleaned lawns at the Country Club. The two boys avoided the gangs and the *tecatos,* drug users. He went to bebop dances in the gym, and recalls listening to music by Bill Haley and the Comets and Fats Domino. Baseball was popular in summer, and football reigned supreme in the fall.

In his autobiography, he remembers driving customized '48 Fords, learning to French kiss, and discovering the meaning of "going all the way" with girls. In the barrio, he saw the *vatos,* or dudes, dressed in tapered denims and black shoes with double soles. The most popular hairstyle was the ducktail. He recalls, "we were all pretending, growing up and pretending we were as cool as Jimmy Dean. We pretended to know everything, and we didn't." The young boy who had suffered a near-death experience was now a teenager on his way to Albuquerque High School.

In high school, Rudolfo Anaya made good grades, but he states in his autobiography that he did not distinguish himself. He recalls reading *Reader's Digest* during free period in English class, and has fond memories of Albuquerque in the 1950s. Like most teenagers, he listened to the music of Elvis Presley. Every Saturday afternoon, he would go to the Kimo Theater to watch movies such as *The Blackboard Jungle* (1955) and *Rebel Without a Cause* (1954). The atmosphere was filled with the music of legendary performers such as Richie Valens, the Platters, Chuck Berry, and Connie Francis. With his friends, he would hang around Lionel's, a local drive-in, and attend dances at the local community center.

Rudy Anaya, Class of '56, Albuquerque High School.

One interesting part of Anaya's life at this time is his decision to become a writer. "I became a writer in my childhood," he writes in his autobiography. He recalls his teen years in Albuquerque. Little was taught to Mexican Americans about their history or literature. There were few Mexican teachers who could serve as role models and mentors. As a result, few students entered professional fields after graduation from high school.

But there was one important facet that he recalls—the stories that he heard from his family. These *cuentos,* or folktales, spiced his life with excitement and imagination. The community was a natural spring for folklore and mythology. Anaya says that it was during his adolescence that he discovered his artistic soul by noticing brightly painted walls, intricate carvings on door frames, beautifully decorated altars in homes, and the expression of emotion evoked by Mexican music—corridos, boleros, and polkas (*Autobiography,* p. 13). These elements offered him the inspiration needed by a young writer to develop his talent.

After graduation from Albuquerque High School in 1956, Anaya attended Browning Business School for two years. In his autobiography, he mentions that with more study, he would have been a certified public accountant, but found the work unfulfilling. Instead, he dropped out of business college and enrolled in the university. He lacked the financial resources, so he worked hard—in every odd job he could find. He kept the accounting records for a neighborhood bar and later worked for a state agency. His life at this stage was balanced among working long hours, fitting classes into his schedule at the university, and reading into the night.

"We were Mexican students, unprepared by high school to compete as scholars," he says. "We were tolerated rather than accepted." He struggled with his command of English and worked hard to learn the rules. "It was a lonely time; many of us did not survive," he states. Determined to succeed and be accepted, Rudolfo Anaya chose a road not taken by many Mexican-American students who graduated from high school in the 1950s.

Chapter 3

To Sir, With Love:
Anaya as a Young Scholar

"The friendship of other Chicanos helped me survive in
the university."

(Autobiography, p. 14)

At the University of New Mexico, Rudolfo Anaya met
and became friends with other Mexican-American students
who helped him face the rigors of academia. He recalls
studying hard, working his way through school, and associ-
ating with a friend named Dennis Martinez. This young
man became his *compadre,* and Anaya was a *padrino,* or
groomsman, at his wedding.

On weekends, Rudolfo and his friends would get
together, play pool, drink beer, and meet girls. They
enjoyed fishing in the Jemez Mountains. It was also at this
time that Rudolfo Anaya began to move away from the
Catholic church. "Life and the church had betrayed me," he
says. He began to write poetry to fill the void. He fell in love
with a young artist at the university, but she moved away.

"Love is most poignant when we are young... in the tradition of the Beatnik generation which was moving around the country, she moved away. I was shattered."

The 1950s were the age of the Beatniks. This generation would revolutionize the language, literature, clothing, music, and thinking among young people. It was in vogue to attend poetry readings in coffee houses. People of that era remember the clothing trends—berets, black turtleneck sweaters, and sunglasses. Women replaced the short bob with long, straight hair parted in the middle. Men sported long sideburns, goatees, and mustaches. The pompadour made famous by Elvis Presley, Fabian, and Paul Anka disappeared, and haircuts for men featured bangs and longer hair in the back. The Beatles made this style famous a decade later.

James Dean was the movie heartthrob of the day. He represented the rebel without a cause, the non-conformist, the social outcast who lived his life according to his own code. The brooding persona that he portrayed in films such as *East of Eden,* based on John Steinbeck's novel, and *Giant,* adapted from the Edna Ferber classic about the life of Jordan Benedict, a Texas oil baron, made him an icon among young people. Books by Jack Kerouac and Allen Ginsberg were popular during this time.

Questions about teenagers and morality arose when rock-and-roll star Elvis Presley's debut on the famous "Ed Sullivan Show" in 1956 was censored. His dancing on screen was shot from the waist up because censors felt that his hip movements and gestures were suggestive and offensive to viewers.

"I Love Lucy" became the first situation comedy to feature an interracial marriage, this one between an American woman (Lucille Ball) and a Cuban musician (Desi Arnaz). It raised eyebrows among viewers. Desi Arnaz, the mastermind behind the hit show, was the only member of the cast who never received an Emmy nomination. Lucy and Desi's television son, Little Ricky, became the first bi-racial child to be presented to the discerning viewing public.

Dick Clark's famous dance party, "American Bandstand," was the most popular television show for teenagers. They listened to the latest record hits and learned the newest dances such as "The Locomotion" and "The Mashed Potato." Western shows like "Gunsmoke" and "Rawhide," featuring a young Clint Eastwood as Rowdy Yates, drew large viewing audiences. George Reeves drew raves from the younger crowd as he soared through the sky in his role as "Superman." The decade saw people's passion for hula hoops, 3-D films viewed with special glasses, poodle skirts, customized cars, and rock-and-roll. This was the world that Rudolfo Anaya lived in as a teenager.

A decade later, the Beatnik generation would evolve into the "Flower Children," or hippie movement, for teenagers of the '60s and '70s. Two common threads found among young people during these decades were loss of love and faith. Anaya felt both.

To survive, he wrote exclamatory and passionate poetry. He recalls reciting such lines as, "Man is free! But everywhere he is in chains!" by Rousseau. He wrote novels of young people in crisis, much like Holden Caulfield in J.D.

Salinger's *The Catcher in the Rye* and Sonny Crawford in Larry McMurtry's *The Last Picture Show*. He wrote reams of manuscripts and recalls writing a novel that had almost one thousand pages. And like Wilson Rawls, author of such famous children's books as *Where the Red Fern Grows* and *The Summer of the Monkeys,* he burned all those old manuscripts. His writing became an outlet for self-expression and a voice for his emotions.

He received his B.A. degree in English in 1963 and found a teaching position in a small town in New Mexico. From 1963 to 1971, he taught at both the junior high and senior high school levels in Albuquerque. He received a master of arts degree in English from the University of New Mexico in 1968 and served as director of counseling at the University of Albuquerque. In 1972 he completed a master of arts degree in guidance and counseling, also from UNM. Two years later, he began his professorship at the university, teaching creative writing and Chicano Literature.

Anaya states in his autobiography that he did not leave home, except for trips to New Orleans and New York. From these travels, he gathered ideas for writing projects. In 1966 he married Patricia Lawless of Kansas. Of his wife, Anaya says, "I think that she was the one person who truly believed I could be a writer. She became a good editor who could read my work and respond to its strengths and weaknesses."

As Anaya states, "for many writers, marriage is difficult." But he needed a stable base from which to write, so his marriage and home have been positive elements in his life. Speaking candidly, he says that the tragedy of his wife's two miscarriages were the most difficult experiences of his life. With time, he learned to accept what happened and move on with his career. "Still, the image of that loss remains sharp and clear in my mind, painful," he says.

In the 1960s, he threw out all his old work and began to work on his novel, *Bless Me, Ultima.*

Teaching by day, he would write in the afternoon and evening. The plot was simple at first. It was the story of a young boy growing up in a small town in New Mexico. To add realism to the novel, Rudolfo went back to his childhood and recalled his upbringing by Rafaelita and Martin Anaya. Many of Tony Marez's experiences in the story mirror his own.

It was not easy for him to weave the story because he had not developed his writing voice yet. He was imitating a style and mode which did not correspond to the people and environment of Pastura and Santa Rosa.

With no role models to inspire him, Rudolfo Anaya set out to become a writer. As an English major, he had read classics by Chaucer, Shakespeare, Milton, and Dante. American authors captivated his attention, but as he states in his autobiography, "Even Faulkner, with his penchant for the fantastic world of the South, could not help me in Mexican/Indian New Mexico. I would have to find my own way alone" (p. 16). With no formal training or background in professional writing and publishing, he began to write a manuscript that would change his destiny forever. Like a young tenor who practices to develop his singing range,

Rudolfo Anaya was perfecting his writing voice. His debut as a novelist would follow after a long period of steady writing and rewriting.

In an interview with John F. Crawford (*Conversations With Rudolfo Anaya, 1996*), Anaya discusses his experiences as a beginning writer: "... in the sixties when I first began to work, I used Anglo American writers as role models. But I really couldn't get my act together until I left them behind. They had a lot to teach me and I don't underestimate that—you're learning whether you're reading a comic book or Hemingway or Shakespeare or Cervantes—but I couldn't tell my story in their terms" (p. 108).

Ultima stepped into his life and opened his eyes to his *own* universe. He created the novel by thinking in Spanish and writing in English. His life was about to change totally with the publication of his famous book. *Bless Me, Ultima* was about to take center stage.

Chapter 4

The Genesis of a Chicano Classic

"I was working late one night, trying to breathe life into the novel that would one day be known as *Bless Me, Ultima* . . . I heard a noise and turned to see the old woman dressed in black enter the room. This is how Ultima came to me . . ."

(Autobiography, p. 16)

With these words, Rudolfo Anaya explains the source of inspiration for *Bless Me, Ultima*. He was typing one night and suddenly felt the presence of an old woman in his room. She asks, *"Que haces, hijo?* What are you doing, my son?" Anaya answers that he is writing a story. The woman taps his shoulder and he feels the power of the *remolino,* or whirlwind. He closes his eyes and has a vision of the story.

Many of his associates have asked him if he was drinking or hallucinating when he saw the famous vision. Using his trademark wit, Rudolfo Anaya responds that he was not drinking, despite his affinity for good bourbon or scotch. He affirms that he never drinks when he writes. Always committed to his work, he refuses to walk the path that many writers discover when they achieve a certain level of fame. They do and say things which will enhance their notoriety. He believes in writing and rewriting until the work is solid in style and form—and ready for submission to the publishers.

"I worked for seven years on *Bless Me, Ultima,*" said Anaya during a teleconference with my Chicano Literature class on November 30, 1998. While teaching in the Albuquerque public schools by day, he wrote the novel at night. The old woman opened his eyes to the reality of life and the roots of his soul. He discovered that he could express himself without imitating the writers whose works he read as a teenager. He wrote as Rudolfo Anaya—the *"Nuevo Mexicano, indio, catolico, hispano...* son of my mother and father, son of the earth which nurtured me, son of my community, son of my people," he writes in his autobiography (p. 17). He adds that he learned plotlines from the movie matinees at the Kimo Theater on Saturday afternoons and from the comic books he read as a young boy. To him, everything he had experienced had value. Nothing was lost.

As the novel neared completion, Anaya found himself caught in the turmoil of the Vietnam War and the whirlwind of the Chicano Movement. In California, Cesar Chávez led *huelgas,* or strikes, and formed the farm workers' union. In New Mexico, Reyes Lopez Tijerina awakened the spirit of people who were involved in the now-famous Tierra Amarilla courthouse raid. These individuals began to learn *la tristeza,* or sadness, stemming from the loss of ancestral lands of the old Mexican and Spanish land grants. Corky Gonzalez formed the Crusade for Justice in Denver, Colorado. In Texas, the Raza Unida Party was formed, and Ramsey Muniz made history by becoming the first Chicano to run for governor of the Lone Star State in 1969.

On November 22, 1963, President John F. Kennedy was assassinated in Dallas, plunging the country into a time of grief. Chicano communities throughout the Southwest were affected deeply. Many Hispanic Catholics placed pictures of President Kennedy in their altars at home amidst flowers, rosaries, and candles. *Corridos,* or ballads, of the Kennedy legacy were written and played on Spanish radio stations throughout the Southwest.

Bless Me, Ultima

Rudolfo Anaya wrote incessantly during this turbulent era. He wrote daily, unlike some of the young writers at the university who wrote sporadically. In essence, he created his own spirit. After completing *Bless Me, Ultima,* he began to circulate it. With no prior experience in publishing, he thought that a young writer could only realize his dream by approaching trade publishers in New York. But things were changing. "Little did I know that many of the giants of the publishing world were dying, that American publishing was changing, that the small presses of the country were on their way to creating a publishing revolution," he recalls.

He circulated *Ultima* among numerous New York publishing houses. "I collected enough form letter rejections to wallpaper the proverbial room, but was undaunted," he says. In 1971 he discovered a journal entitled *El Grito,* a Chicano quarterly, founded by Professor Octavio Romano, Herminio Rios, and associates at the University of California at Berkeley. In it was a call for manuscripts. Anaya wrote a letter to the editors and they responded. They wanted to see the novel. After a few months, he heard from them—they wanted to publish it!

Bless Me, Ultima appeared on the market in 1972 and was welcomed with critical acclaim. It was awarded the prestigious Premio Quinto Sol for the best novel written by a Chicano. Rudolfo Anaya went to Berkeley and met Octavio Romano, Herminio Rios, and Andres Ybarra, three key figures in the establishment of the fledgling Quinto Sol Publications.

The novel became an instant success. It was featured in Chicano Studies programs throughout the Southwest. The story of Tony Marez and his life in Guadalupe, New Mexico, during the 1940s captivated the attention of all Chicanos.

At home, with painting of Ultima in background.

Teachers in the public schools wanted to use it in their classes, in spite of censorship that was holding back the introduction of Chicano Literature into the curricula.

University professors read and quoted passages from it in American Literature and sociology seminars. People in the *barrios* embraced the story because they could relate to it—action, language, characters, and themes.

Ultima represented the *curanderas,* or faith healers, who cured people of their ills when there were no medical doctors or hospitals in the rural areas of the Southwest. Her knowledge of medicinal herbs made people think of their own *abuelitas* (grandmothers) or *parteras* (midwives), who cure *el mal de ojo* (the evil eye) with an egg to cleanse a child's body and mind from evil. Ultima became mother, grandmother, godmother, and shaman to the Marez family and the people of Guadalupe who believed in her inner strength.

The elements surrounding the small town reminded people of their own hometowns. Readers laughed at the antics of the gang—Bones, Horse, Abel, Cico, Florence, Jason, Samuel, the Vitamin Kid, and Tony. But they held their breath when they saw the dark side of characters such as Tenorio Trementina and his daughters, who are rumored to dance with the devil in the depths of the river forest. Guadalupe is the microcosm of the world which Tony Marez discovers.

The presence of Our Lady of Guadalupe in the Marez family was felt in the hearts of all Hispanic Catholics. Tony's holy communion on Easter Sunday reminds Hispanic Catholics of that special day in the lives of little girls in white dresses and veils and little boys in suits and neckties who receive the body of Christ for the first time.

Anaya's blend of English and Spanish is effective in presenting the two worlds of the Chicanos of Aztlan. He is one of the first Chicano writers to combine both languages. The language used by the characters is *Chiconics,* a term I coined in writing an article for *The Journal of Big Bend Studies* (Volume IX, 1997). Using the vernacular of *la Chicanada,* or the Mexican-American population, Anaya gives a realistic sound to the novel. Readers hear it in the voice of Ultima as she speaks to Tony about the ways of men. And they cringe with fear as they hear it in the piercing screams of Tenorio Trementina when he attacks Tony and threatens to destroy Ultima.

Bless Me, Ultima is hailed by literary critics as Anaya's opus of Chicano life and culture. It has everything from the gentility of Miss Maestas, Tony's first-grade teacher, to the charisma of Father Brynes, who represents the force of the Catholic church in the lives of Mexican people. Tony's lunch of *frijoles* and *chile* reflects the humble nourishment of lower socio-economic families who cannot afford to pay for the proverbial meal cards in public school cafeterias. His awareness of *la tristeza de la vida* after being ridiculed by his classmates for being different makes many people think of their first day of school. Tony's ostracism by his classmates mirrors the injustices suffered by minority children in public schools across the United States. In short, the novel awakens the senses of young readers to the realities of life. That is one of the main reasons for its success and popularity with students and teachers alike.

All of a sudden, Rudolfo Anaya was traveling throughout the country. He found himself in California, Washington, D.C., Texas, Colorado, Michigan, and Ohio. Large groups of Chicanos lived in these states and were ready to read the literature that reflected their lives and culture. This was Anaya's hour of triumph. He captured this feeling in one of my favorite passages from his autobiography: "It was a fabulous time to be alive. I was a novelist, a novelist whose work had been awarded a literary prize, an honor which carries great distinction in the literary world. Everywhere I went, I was lionized. It was exhilarating" (p. 19).

The writer had stepped into the literary world he was helping to create. Nothing had been lost.

Chapter 5

Rudolfo Anaya and the Chicano Literary Movement

"I made my connection with the Chicano Movement...
the winds of change, which before had only been felt
as the stirring of the storm, were now a gale of com-
mitment in our people."

(Autobiography, p. 19)

The Chicano Movement began in the mid-1960s and
swept across the Southwest, affecting all aspects of life for
Mexican-American people—political, educational, and eco-
nomic. Chicano Studies classes and programs appeared on
college and university campuses. Students were now able
to study the history, culture, and literature of their Mexican
ancestors. Young authors were writing everywhere, making
Chicano Literature a new facet of American Literature.
Schools were forced to adopt some forms of Chicano
Studies. Changes did not come easy and did not appear
overnight.

Rudolfo Anaya was teaching classes in both junior high

and high school in Albuquerque in the sixties. He met Patricia Lawless at the University of New Mexico. Her parents had moved from Kansas to build their retirement home there. Anaya had visited Taos and had stayed with friends Cruz and Toñita Trujillo. With Cruz, Rudolfo fished and hunted. He began to understand the balance of nature and his appreciation for his Native American background.

Like Nick Adams in Hemingway's famous story, "Big Two-Hearted River," who discovers that nature and man are one after witnessing the atrocities of war, Rudolfo Anaya learned to see the hunt as a ritual that pits man against animal. "A deer is a source of nourishment for the pueblo... a deer is also a brother," he writes. Also like Nick, Anaya felt the healing of the human spirit through the beauty of nature.

After their marriage, Rudolfo and Patricia began to travel in Mexico. Having no family there, they went as

Rudolfo and wife, Patricia, 1970.

tourists first. His roots were in New Mexico, taking him back as far as the famous land grants which had been given to his father's family by the Mexican and Spanish governments. These grants covered large tracts of land along the Rio Grande in Albuquerque's south valley, and extended into the desert as far as the Rio Puerco. "Most of the big land grants were stolen away from the true inheritors," Anaya observes.

Heart of Aztlan

From the knowledge he received from his parents about the land grants, he decided to include similar themes into his second book, *Heart of Aztlan,* published in 1976. Like the Anaya family, the central characters live in the Barelas barrio in Albuquerque. The disintegration of the Chicano family is seen in the children of Clemente Chavez and his wife, Adelita. One of the sons, Benjie, turns to drugs and alcohol and is lost to the streets. The daughters, Ana and Juanita, lose interest in school and become social outcasts. Jason, the middle son, takes over the numerous responsibilities of the family when his father begins to drink heavily. Adelita blames the move from the small town, where her children were born, to the city for the breakup of *la familia.*

The description of the ambience is realistic—crowded barrios, street corner prostitutes, boys trying to be *machos, tecatos* in their lowrider *ranflas,* or customized cars, and the mad scramble of people in search of jobs by pounding the pavement every day. The city and its temptations prove to be fatal to the Chavez family.

This scenario reminds Chicano Literature students of "22 Miles," the famous poem written by Crystal City Chicano writer and political activist, Jose Angel Gutierrez, who is now on the faculty at the University of Texas–Arlington. His classic poem presents a view of a Mexican-American barrio through the eyes of a young man. The character reminds readers of Jason in *Heart of Aztlan* and Florence in *Bless Me, Ultima*. They question the purpose of their existence and the Chicano's struggle to survive in a society full of inequality and social injustice. The miles are symbolic of the years that a Chicano spends discovering himself. In his poem, Jose Angel Gutierrez's descriptions of the barrio have amazing similarities to those created by Rudolfo Anaya in *Heart of Aztlan:* "pretty people, combed and squeaky clean, on arrowlike roads/ Pregnant girls, ragged brats, swarthy machos, rosary beads/ and friends waddle clumsily over and across hills, each other/ mud, cold, and woods on caliche ruts" (*Literatura Chicana: Texto y Contexto,* p. 270). Another line that reminds the readers of Tony's first day of school and his lunch of *frijoles* and green *chile* reads as follows in Gutierrez's poem: "You know... chorizo tacos and tortillas ARE good, even at school. Speaking Spanish is a talent" (*Literatura Chicana,* p. 270).

Through characters such as Crispin, the blind poet, Anaya incorporates the presence of the myths and legends of Indian Mexico. This theme was prevalent during the Chicano Movement. It became an obsession for writers to study their genealogy in the same manner as Alex Haley did with *Roots,* his famous novel that presented African-

American culture and history through the eyes of the young black slave named Kunta Kinte. The narrator relates the story of his ancestors before being brought to America on a slave ship and the aftermath.

The term "Negro," which had been used for centuries in regards to people of African-American descent, evolved into "Black American" or "African American" in the decades following the signing of the Civil Rights Bill in 1964. Likewise, the word *mestizo* appeared and was used to identify Chicanos with a blend of both Spanish, Mexican, and Indian bloodlines. Mural art became popular throughout the Southwest and portrayed the different facets of Chicano culture—history, religion, and language.

In California, Luis Valdez founded El Teatro Campesino, the farm workers' theater, and presented classic satires such as *Las Dos Caras Del Patroncito* ("The Two Faces of the Boss"), *Los Vendidos* ("The Sellouts"), and *The Dark Root of the Scream*. *Zoot Suit* introduced the world of the *pachuco*, or homeboy, to American society. It was so popular that it opened on Broadway and had a very successful run in Los Angeles. The movie version with Edward James Olmos in the title role became an important film for its depiction of Chicano life in the barrios of Los Angeles. The overall message was clear—Chicanos were developing their artistic voices in different genres, voices, and mediums. However, they did encounter opposition and criticism for their work.

One interesting note that Rudolfo Anaya presents in his autobiography is his reference to the small band of Marxist-Leninist critics who tore apart any type of Chicano

Literature that did not focus on the struggle of the poor people fighting capitalism. Anaya states, *"Bless Me, Ultima was attacked by the Marxist critics as having no relevant social value to the working class."* But his fans came to his defense and *Ultima* survived. It became an anthem for Chicano Literature.

Anaya then began to write *Heart of Aztlan,* the second novel of the trilogy. In *Heart of Aztlan,* Anaya was passionate about presenting the strong bond between people and the land that was once theirs. The land known as the Southwest was once Aztlan, the territory from which the natives drew their strength and nourishment. In the 1970s, Anaya visited the ruins of Tenochtitlan, Cholula, and Monte Alban. He read extensively about the Indian history of Mexico. The concept of using Aztlan as a central theme in his work was very strong.

Anaya accepting Premio Quinto Sol Award, Berkeley, California.

Incidentally, Anaya was in Mexico City in the summer of 1974 when he received a call from the chairman of the English Department at the University of New Mexico. He was offered a position as professor of creative writing. He accepted and returned to Albuquerque to begin a tenure that would span two decades. Nothing had been lost.

It was also during this year that he was invited to serve

on the board of the Coordinating Council of Literary Magazines (CCLM), with offices in New York. He was now in a position to meet influential people in the publishing world and well-known writers such as Ishmael Reed and Toni Cade Bambara. With this appointment, he was given a chance to travel throughout the country. Anaya recalls his visits to North and South Carolina, Atlanta, Seattle, Los Angeles, and Buffalo, saying, "we took our show on the road and became a very active part of one of the most phenomenal movements of the country: the small press revolution" (*Autobiography,* p. 22).

This was a time of change. Writers of Mexican-American, Native-American, African-American, and Asian-American backgrounds surfaced and published novels, short story and poetry anthologies, dramas, screenplays, children's books, and journals. Anaya made lifelong friends with some of these men and women who were proponents of minority literature in America. He states, "We were the vanguard of something new and exciting, as was the women writers' movement" (p. 23).

Tortuga

In the late 1970s, Anaya began to write *Tortuga,* the third novel of the trilogy. It was a novel based on his own hospital stay when he was injured in a diving accident. He states that the novel was a most difficult project to write because he drew ideas from painful scenes in his adolescence and his near-death experience.

In the story, he creates a young man who is admitted

to a hospital with a broken back. He is placed in a body cast which makes him look like a turtle, hence the title of the novel. Once there, he begins to heal and is able to get on his feet after weeks of treatment and therapy. Tortuga discovers the "lifers" who will never see the world outside the hospital walls. "I took my characters to the depths of despair and human suffering..." he writes in his autobiography (p. 23).

Writing *Tortuga* was therapeutic for Anaya. He had created characters who remind readers of the social outcasts found in Ken Kesey's *One Flew Over the Cuckoo's Nest.* The hospital is a vision of an *infierno,* or hell. Tortuga, like Randle Patrick McMurphy, becomes a hero to the young men and women who are looking for a way to heal their physical and emotional wounds. "Perhaps I was finally bringing together my own foundations of faith, finally regrouping from an existential wasteland and giving form to my own credo," he writes (p. 23).

The publication of *Tortuga* marked the end of a busy decade for Rudolfo Anaya. Anaya collaborated on a screenplay entitled "Bilingualism: Promise for Tomorrow," with Carlos Penichet and Jeff Penichet for Bilingual Education Services in 1976. In the 1980s, he would carry his writing talents into other genres—drama, short fiction, historical fiction, and children's literature.

Rafaelita Anaya's vision of her son as a writer had come true.

Chapter 6

The Decade of the Hispanics

"My discipline as a writer evolved from early training.
I would write every morning, and I still do. I traveled
to explore the world and ventured out to do readings,
but I would always return to home base."

(*Autobiography,* p. 24)

By the dawn of the 1980s, often regarded as the "Decade of the Hispanics," Rudolfo Anaya's talent as a writer was recognized throughout the country. He was invited to read at the White House during the Carter Administration as part of "A Salute to American Poets and Writers." Many awards were bestowed upon him during this time: The National Endowment for the Arts Fellowship (1979, 1980); The National Chicano Council for Higher Education Fellowship (1980); The Kellogg Foundation Fellowship (1983-86); and the New Mexico Governor's Award for Excellence in Literature.

His work during this time took a different route. With his colleague, Jose Griego y Maestas, he wrote and translated a collection of folktales entitled *Cuentos: Tales from the Hispanic Southwest.* The book captivated attention with its bilingual text, interesting drawings, and glossary of English/Spanish terms. He co-edited an anthology called *Ceremony of Brotherhood.* His well known collection of short fiction, *Silence of the Llano,* was published in 1982.

Another anthology, *Cuentos Chicanos,* published in 1983, opens with Anaya's popular short story, "B. Traven is Alive and Well in Cuernavaca," and features an impressive honor roll of writers: Denise Chavez, Ron Arias, Ana Castillo, Nash Candelaria, Sergio Elizondo, Tino Villanueva, Mario Suarez, and Marta Salinas. Some of the stories are written in English and Spanish. The short stories present a wide variety of themes, ranging from barrio life as seen in "El Tonto del Barrio" by José Armas and "Willow Game" by Denise Chavez, to the struggles of migrant workers in "The Circuit" by Francisco Jimenez.

La Llorona

In 1984 Rudolfo Anaya wrote *The Legend of La Llorona,* a novella based on the research of the ancient story. "To write her story," writes Anaya in his autobiography, "I went back to the Mexico of Cortes and the conquest of Mexico. The heroine becomes Malinche who befriends Cortes and is later betrayed by him." Chicanos who grew up listening to the chilling tale of *La Llorona,* as told by Guelo and Guela, Grandpa and Grandma, were impressed to see the story in print.

Malinche has come to mean traitor in Mexico. In my own home, my mother would use the word *"malinche"* in reference to a treacherous woman. *La Llorona* was told in

Spanish-speaking homes as a *fabula,* or fable, that presented a moral to young listeners. The troubled woman killed her child in a fit of anger and was destined to spend the rest of her life weeping about her fate. Like Medea from Greek mythology and Lady Macbeth from the Elizabethan period, *Llorona* is a classic story of a tragic heroine who falls from grace and pays the consequences of her crime.

It was the ultimate horror story to relate at night around the kitchen table as Hispanic women like my sainted mother made *pan dulce* (sweet bread) and embroidered doilies and pillow cases. *La Llorona* and many other folktales, such as *"El Chupacabras,"* were part of the oral literary tradition for centuries but had never been captured in print in the style of Rudolfo Anaya. The book's cover attracts attention with its depiction of Malinche standing between Cortes and Montezuma, *el español y el indio,* with Aztec art as background. Students of Mexican descent know the story very well and enjoy reading different versions found throughout the Southwest.

In fact, the story is so popular that an annual festival honoring *La Llorona* is held at Rio Gallinas, Las Vegas, New Mexico. Historians, folklorists, and writers travel from all over the country to attend the festival and hear a variety of papers read about the legend. The conference also features music, dramatic productions, and artwork based on the folktale.

Juan Chicaspatas

The Adventures of Juan Chicaspatas, an epic poem, was published in 1985. In this piece, the two characters, Juan

Chicaspatas and his compadre, Al Penco, travel through Aztlan in search of adventure, much like Don Quixote and Sancho Panza did in the classic work written by Miguel de Cervantes Saavedra during the Ciglo de Oro, the Golden Age of Spanish Literature.

In Anaya's poem, one of the characters is asked to recite a poem and he does. The characters of the poem then evolve into those of the story that Rudolfo Anaya was weaving into a novel. The two protagonists, Juan Chicaspatas, and his compadre, Al Penco, travel back to Mexico, or Aztlan, to seek knowledge and understanding of their identity and past.

A Chicano in China

From his journey to the Far East in 1984, Anaya wrote *A Chicano in China,* a travel journal. He had a lifelong dream to travel there and find the common threads that exist between the Chinese and Chicano cultures. He describes the dragons as Quetzalcoatl. The lakes and ponds hold the mysterious origins of the famous Legend of the Golden Carp found in *Bless Me, Ultima,* and in the Chinese peasants, Anaya sees his grandfather's face. This book is excellent for use in social studies and multicultural studies classes in junior high and senior high schools.

Lord of the Dawn: The Legend of Quetzalcoatl

His travels during this decade took him to many foreign countries. He lectured in Israel, Paris, and Bordeaux, France. Anaya wrote *Lord of the Dawn: The Legend of Quetzalcoatl,* a historical novel, based on the enduring epic myth of Mesoamerica. Quetzalcoatl is depicted as a man of peace who comes to the Toltecs to teach them art, agriculture, and harmony with the universe. As he did with *Llorona*, Rudolfo Anaya was bringing the literary history of *los indios* in Mexico into perspective. *Lord of the Dawn* creates an interest in the *mestizo* roots of Chicanos living in the Southwest.

New Directions in Genre

An illustrated children's story, *The Farolitos of Christmas*, was published in 1987 and was presented as a play by a theatrical group called "La Compania." The compelling story of two young girls, Luz and Reina, and their respective wishes for Christmas make the book a must for elementary teachers who are looking for literature that celebrates the Hispanic celebration of Christmas. In 1999 the story of Abuelo and Luz continues in *Farolitos for Abuelo,* as Abuelo saves a young man from drowning in the river and loses his own life when he contracts pneumonia from the bone-chilling waters. The image of the *farolitos,* or little lights, is a focal point in both books.

Anaya edited *Voces: An Anthology of Nuevo Mexicano Writers* and wrote a drama entitled *Who Killed Don Jose?* during this time. He further edited two anthologies: a collection of short fiction called *Tierra: Contemporary Short Fiction of New Mexico* and *Aztlan: Essays on the Chicano Homeland,* which he co-edited with Francisco Lomeli. He delivered the 34th Annual Research Lecture at the University of New Mexico and lectured in Egypt in 1989.

Signing books at
Squaw Valley Writers Conference.

By the end of the decade, Rudolfo Anaya had evolved into a prolific writer, lecturer, and world traveler. Two milestones in his life came when he received an honorary Doctor of Humane Letters from the University of Albuquerque (1981) and an honorary Doctor of Humane Letters from Marycrest College, Davenport, Iowa (1984). He has been awarded five more honorary Doctorates of Humane Letters— The College of Santa Fe (1991); University of New England (1992); California Lutheran University (1994); University of New Mexico, *honoris causa* (1996) and the University of New Hampshire (1997).

In the last decade of the millennium, Anaya would make some changes in his professional life and would pleasantly surprise his reading audience by writing in a different literary genre. Also, he would begin to write a novel about the city, a task that would take almost a decade to complete. This novel would lead him into a different literary genre—the mystery thriller and the appearance of the Anaya hero named Sonny Baca.

Chapter 7

Godfather of Chicano Literature

"I think I've always had readership in many communi-
ties. Now that I have a New York publisher (Warner
Books), I have more distribution, so that accounts for
a lot of new interest in my work."
("NM Author Completes Tetralogy," *El Paso Times,*
August 10, 1997, 6B)

The 1990s brought important changes and achieve-
ments to Rudolfo Anaya's life. In 1992 he completed a book
that he had started several years before. In a book entitled
Conversations with Rudolfo Anaya, edited by Bruce Dick and
Silvio Sirias (University Press of Mississippi, 1998), Anaya
says, "(it) was difficult in the sense that I worked on the
novel for ten years.... But I constantly worked on
Alburquerque during those years. The changes in subject
matter and style were not easy. They were earned" (p. 158).

Alburquerque

The novel *Alburquerque* attracted attention because the
themes were different from those found in his early works.

41

"The lyricism I had when I was younger is not as prevalent," he tells Ray Gonzalez in an interview entitled "Songlines of the Southwest" (Bloomsbury Review, 1993) published in *Conversations* (153). Anaya attacks the political system found within the infrastructure of the city. Questions arise within the power structure of the urban areas. Urban development becomes a nightmare to an indigenous culture. The use of high-powered technology in laboratories confuse and scare those individuals who do not comprehend the spectrum of scientific research and its perimeters. One major focus is the controversy over water usage and who will control the use of water in the future.

The spelling of "Albuquerque" puzzles people as they read the novel. Is it true that the word was painted by an Anglo station master on a railroad sign in the 1880s and forgot to trill the first "r"? Rudolfo Anaya opens the novel with the legend behind the spelling of the word. Set in the present time, the novel features the central character, Abran Gonzalez, who is looking for his father in the dangerous streets of Albuquerque. He meets Ben Chavez, a writer who makes a lasting impression on the young man, and opens his eyes to the realities of life. Anaya assembles an impressive cast of characters in this novel, including Frank Dominic, an evil lawyer, who intends to rechannel the waters of the Rio Grande and turn the downtown area into a desert Venice. Also in the plot are the people of the city and the small towns of the surrounding area. The city and its industry are important to those who depend on their work for survival. Dominic's destructive plans will affect many people's lives.

Alburquerque, published in 1992, was a difficult novel for Anaya to write because it was a departure from the style and voice he had used in *Bless Me, Ultima, Heart of Aztlan,* and *Tortuga.* This book presents strong political undertones and unveiled environmental issues. It became the first part of a quartet which would combine Anaya's famous magical realism and contemporary themes involving power struggle, espionage, death, vengeance, racial tensions, and the age-old struggle between good and evil.

The novel received good reviews. According to writer Ishmael Reed, "*Alburquerque* is more than a novel about romantic and political intrigue and changing demographics in the Southwest. In this novel by a world-class author, Mr. Anaya uses *Alburquerque* as a symbol of the issues that Americans must face in the twenty-first century." Juan Bruce-Novoa, who interviewed Anaya for his book, *Chicano Authors: Interview by Inquiry,* lauds the novel as "Anaya's best work since *Ultima.*" John Nichols, author of such noted southwestern novels as *The Milagro Beanfield War,* gives the novel a glowing review: "Above all, in this novel is a deep caring for the land and culture and for the spiritual well-being of people, environment, landscape.... Rudy Anaya obviously loves Albuquerque, a city rich in tradition, full of flaws, full of wonder."

Zia Summer

Anaya followed *Alburquerque* with an action-packed novel entitled *Zia Summer.* In it, he introduces private detective Sonny Baca, who investigates a series of murder crimes in the city. In "An Interview with Rudolfo Anaya" (*Conversations*), Bruce Dick and Silvio Sirias discuss the creation of Sonny Baca with the author. Sirias asks, "Speaking of characters, would you consider Sonny Baca to be the most memorable character since Ultima?" Anaya replies, "I think that in a strange way he will become the most memorable since the Antonio-Ultima pair in *Bless Me, Ultima.*" (p. 179).

In *Zia Summer,* gumshoe Sonny Baca is the great-grandson of Elfego Baca, whose role as a sheriff in New Mexico made him legendary. Like his *bisabuelo,* or great-grandfather, Sonny carries the traditional Colt .45 and has big dreams. His life is somewhat mundane, handling small cases involving insurance claims and divorces. Suddenly, his cousin, Gloria Dominic, is murdered. Her body is drained of its blood, and the Zia sun symbol is found etched around her navel. The mystery intensifies when Sonny hears that there are several cases of cattle mutilation in the area, and the animals have been drained of their blood as well.

The reader is pulled into the intense world of Sonny Baca as he searches for Gloria's murderer. Rita, Sonny's girlfriend, is at his side as he combs the city for clues. The novel is coated with overtones of political corruption and racial tensions between Chicanos and Anglos. Sonny's investigation leads him back into history, to the pagan rituals practiced by the Aztecas in Mexico before the arrival of the Spaniards. They offered blood to their Sun god. Could Gloria's death be linked to the actions of evil *brujas,* or witches? The reader has to understand the symbolism behind the *Zia,* the sun symbol. As with many of Anaya's books, the historical and cultural perspectives are very strong.

Published in 1993, *Zia Summer* became a page-turner for *aficionados,* or fans, of Rudolfo Anaya's fiction. Writers Max Evans, Robert J. Conley, Judith Van Gieson, and Sandra West Prowell make interesting comments about the book, but the most attractive and often-quoted is the one written by Tony Hillerman: "Anaya, godfather and guru of Chicano Literature, proves he's just as good in the murder mystery field in *Zia Summer.*" The novel proved Anaya's versatility as a writer. His reading public appreciated his desire to explore other genres and write in the realms of magical realism, historical fiction, and mystery thriller fiction.

Rio Grande Fall

Three years later, Anaya published the third novel of the Albuquerque quartet and called it *Rio Grande Fall.* The backdrop of the story is the annual Hot Air Balloon Fiesta of Albuquerque. In the early scenes, a body falls from the sky. The dead woman is the key witness against the villainous Raven, Sonny Baca's nemesis, who is being implicated in the murder of Gloria Dominic.

Four black feathers, Raven's infamous "calling card," are found around the body. Another balloonist is killed by a sniper's bullet, and the committee responsible for staging the Fiesta makes Sonny Baca a tremendous offer to find the killers. He begins a methodical investigation and uncovers some strange events.

Sonny learns a big shipment of cocaine and heroin is being sent to Albuquerque during the festival. In reality, Raven is being used by the drug lords as a distraction. Knowing that Raven has powers that are almost impossible to challenge, Sonny sets out to fight him. Raven can call on his "*tla-huel-puchi*" or animal spirit. To succeed, Sonny seeks the aid of a *curandera,* or faith healer. His guardians will be the coyotes.

The struggle between Sonny Baca and Raven is the central focus of the novel, but there are other themes of importance too. Within the depths of the story, the reader finds the "night faces" of drug lords who use their shipments of narcotics to draw people into their claws and control them. The power of Raven is evident with an ancient evil power that seeks to destroy the universe.

Rudolfo Anaya's use of magical realism is paramount in this novel. The hypnotic effect of the Hot Air Balloon Festival is combined with the realism of death and revenge. Sonny Baca finds that he needs to go back in time and find answers to questions that will help him defeat his nemesis. He hears the story of *brujas* (witches) from the *curandera* who speaks of the mountain called "La Malintzi," an extinct volcano. It is there that *brujas* can transform themselves into their animal forms.

Sonny uncovers this important information from his conversation with the *curandera* about the *tla-huel-puchi*. These notes take the reader back to the days of the Aztec empire before the arrival of the Spaniards. Sonny Baca has to learn the strong powers among the Aztecs in regards to transformations and rituals. Once he unravels Raven's background and his source of strength, Sonny is ready to confront him. When he discovers that his girlfriend, Rita, has fallen into Raven's clutches, Sonny Baca goes after Raven with a vengeance.

Rio Grande Fall drew praise from reviewers in newspapers and magazines across the country. *Hispanic* calls Rudolfo Anaya's book "an exquisitely woven and engrossing detective novel." *Publishers Weekly* says, "A memorable cast of locals . . . . But best here is Sonny's convincing attachment to the land and the traditions that have shaped him."

Perhaps the best review is the one written by Marilyn Staslo, *New York Times Book Review,* who states: "There are stories within stories in this narrative. Some of them are ancient and mystical, others are contemporary and realistic. In Mr. Anaya's incantory voice, they are all magical." *Publishers Weekly* adds, "Anaya has created an easygoing and amiable detective in Sonny Baca, a fellow we should see more of in the future." The *El Paso Times* calls Rudolfo Anaya "one of the best writers in the country."

Shaman Winter

To complete the cycle of the seasons, Anaya wrote *Shaman Winter,* published in 1999. As the novel opens, readers find Sonny Baca confined to a wheelchair. He has strange dreams that carry him back to 1598, when Owl Woman enters New Mexico with Juan de Oñate and his colonists. She is an angel of peace and carries a beautiful bowl that is a Calendar of Dreams. Before she can bring it to her groom on her wedding night, Owl Woman is abducted by none other than Raven, the Bringer of Curses.

From Don Eliseo, a wise, elderly man, Sonny learns that Owl Woman is his ancestor, and Raven has entered his dreams to destroy his history. The horrible nightmares grow, and Sonny's ancestors begin to disappear with each dream. There is only one way for Sonny to fight Raven—to be initiated into the realm of the spirit.

Anaya combines Sonny's dream life to his waking life by having him investigate the disappearance of the Santa Fe mayor's daughter. The four black feathers are found on the missing young woman's pillow. Before long, another young woman is reported missing. It is up to Sonny Baca to find them before Raven kills them. After a horrible encounter with the villain, Sonny saves Rita and speaks to her in the hospital about Raven's demise. Sonny talks about marriage, children, and his ideas about quitting his detective work and possibly returning to teaching. The novel ends with the words *amor y esperanza,* love and hope, and the dawn of a new dream.

According to the *Houston Chronicle,* the novel "blends magic realism with the earthiness of good crime fiction." The *Washington Post* states that "Anaya has created an easygoing and amiable character in Sonny Baca, a fellow we should see more of in the future." The attractive copper-colored book jacket, featuring a beautiful illustration of the mysterious bowl that Owl Woman carries with her as a Calendar of Dreams, is reminiscent of other famous folktales with important symbols that young readers encounter—Pandora's box, Aladdin's magic lamp, Excalibur, the Holy Grail, Penelope's tapestry, and Jason's golden fleece.

With the publication of *Shaman Winter,* Anaya's reading public saw the character of Sonny Baca complete the cycle of the seasons. The imagery and magical realism found in the quartet are part of Anaya's penchant for writing. People who have followed his literature from *Bless Me, Ultima* to Sonny Baca can see common threads—the use of dreams, folklore, history, and magic.

What will he write in the next century? In a teleconference with my Chicano Literature class in 1998, Anaya mentioned an adolescent novel he is writing. Furthermore, he spoke about two children's books that he is creating and an essay that he submitted to the *American Literary Quarterly* and published by Oxford Press. He always has several projects on the drawing board. While working on a longer manuscript, he maintains a balance by writing shorter pieces—essays and children's books.

Although retired from his professorship at UNM, Rudolfo Anaya will never retire from the writing life.

Chapter 8

The Drama of the Nineties

"My writing is on-going. It fills my life."
(*Autobiography*, p. 26)

With these words, Rudolfo Anaya ends the short auto-biographical sketch he published nearly fourteen years ago. He has continued to write in another genre—drama. He explains his interest in drama: "I am now spending more time writing plays, learning techniques of writing drama" (p. 25). In the previous decade, he wrote *The Season of La Llorona* (1980), *The Farolitos of Christmas* (first written as a short story and performed as a play by La Compania in 1987), and *Who Killed Don Jose?* (1987).

Matachines

Matachines, written in 1992, is set in Plaza Vieja, a Hispanic community full of traditions which they share with their neighbors, the Pueblo Indians. The dance of *los Matachines* is full of pageantry, color, and symbolism, combining the beauty of the culture and the tragedy that falls on

Plaza Vieja during the traditional dance of the *Monarca*. The play opens with a scene between the villainous young man named Andres and his aunt, a *bruja*, or witch, who promises to help him win the love of the beautiful Cristina. Andres kills Lorenzo, her boyfriend, as part of his plan to possess Cristina. He appears dressed as el Toro for the dance with Cristina, portraying Malinche in a white lace dress. As he tries to conquer the young woman and denounce Don Patricio, her father, for killing his father years before, Andres loses his life at the hands of Zonzo, the town's simpleton, who stabs him with a cross, screaming, "I killed the diablo..." In the last scene of the play, Teresa, a mute girl, regains her ability to speak and identifies Andres as Lorenzo's killer.

Ay, Compadre

Ay, Compadre premiered in Denver's "El Centro, Su Teatro" and presents the lives of two couples who are experiencing midlife crises. Anaya was interviewed by Ruben Sosa Villegas in 1994 about the play, and Anaya offers this insight about the characters and their conflicts: "They've done a lot of things together and traveled together. And they get along very well, but they're at a point of going through midlife crisis. The women have gone through menopause and the men are going through male menopause" (*Conversations,* p. 161). When asked how he thought the reading audience would react to a play that explores sexuality, Anaya states that the world of sexuality is very open now, especially with the AIDS awareness programs being presented all over the world.

51

Ay, Compadre has a cast reminiscent of *Who's Afraid of Virginia Woolf,* written by Edward Albee, who won the Pulitzer Prize in 1966 for the play and its absurd humor.

Anaya found the inspiration for the play after he visualized a scene in which two couples are playing cards and making hamburgers on the grill. "It's a comedy," he says, "it's a way of looking at the subject matter and bringing it out in public but at the same time treating it in a light-hearted way" (*Conversations,* p. 161).

Billy the Kid

On July 11, 1997, *Billy the Kid* premiered in Albuquerque. Rudolfo Anaya grew up hearing the story of "Billito," the famous outlaw, so it was to be expected that he would write about him. In "Anaya Explores Sexuality, Mid-life in New Play" *(Conversations With Rudolfo Anaya),* Anaya gives Ruben Sosa Villegas background information about *Billy the Kid.* He states: "It's a completely different play because it treats the subject matter—that everyone recognizes Billy the Kid—and we've done it from a Nuevo Mexicano (New Mexican) point of view. We know that Billy the Kid spoke Spanish. He got along well with the Mexicanos of Lincoln County, and I would hear stories when I was a kid about him going to Puerto de Luna where my parents were born and raised" (pp. 162–163).

Angie

Angie opened on July 10, 1998, at La Casa Teatro in Albuquerque, directed by Cecilia Aragon. The plot is the story of an elderly Hispanic woman who moves from her barrio home to a nursing home. As with *Ay, Compadre,* Anaya experiments with another touchy subject among Hispanics—the place of elderly people who have to leave their homes and move into retirement centers because there is no one to take care of them. *Angie* has common threads with Laura Esquivel's 1993 best seller, *Like Water for Chocolate.* The unhappy teenage girl, Tita de la Garza, has to honor a family tradition in which the youngest daughter of a Mexican family will remain at home and care for her aging mother, Mama Elena, a widow with three daughters. Failure to obey the tradition will bring shame and dishonor to Tita and her sisters. Likewise, *Angie* touches the social conscience of people in regards to the lives of the elderly in society.

Jalamanta: A Message from the Desert

In 1996 Anaya published *Jalamanta: A Message from the Desert.* He presents his "eclectic spiritual vision to his readers" in the book, as discussed with Bruce Dick and Silvio Sirias in *Conversations With Rudolfo Anaya* (p. 182). He says that the novel is a reflection of the questions that people have about their place in the universe. "If you look at all of my novels, most of the philosophy of *Jalamanta* has been expressed in them in one way or another," says Anaya, ". . . I am writing about the spirit of people, their soul, their essence" (p. 182).

Bless Me, Ultima was reissued by Warner Books in 1994. When asked if he was going to continue writing for Warner,

Rudolfo Anaya and granddaughter, Kristan.

he said, "Yes. But I publish with other publishers too. For example, my two children's books are published by Hyperion, and I have a couple more in the works. Latino writers have also moved into the area of being represented by agents who are able to gain access to different publishers. So far, however, I am doing very well with Warner Books" (p.182).

With his retirement from teaching in 1993, Rudolfo Anaya now focuses on his writing and lecturing. He attends symposia and lectures on a variety of topics from cultural diversity to creative writing. When asked who his favorite writers are, he refrains from mentioning names because, as he states, "The problem with commenting who your favorite writers that one likes and admires is that you often leave somebody out and then they get their feelings hurt" (*Conversations,* p. 183). He would like to see more fiction writers turn to topics such as art, literature, and philosophy in the new millennium. He would like writers to address questions that people have about life and death. "The older I get the more poignant those questions become," he states (*Conversations,* p. 184).

As he reflects on a career that spans nearly three decades, he sees new horizons for Chicano and Latino writers and their literature. More teachers in the public schools are using multicultural anthologies that have an abundance of poetry, short fiction, drama, and novels written by Chicano, African-American, Native-American, and Asian-American authors. Mainstream publishers are printing more books by Chicano men and women. "I think we have carved an important space for ourselves," he says, "and Latino writers are not only impacting literature. We are influencing art, theater, music" (p. 184). My favorite line in my interview with him was, "We need not to be seen as stereotypes, only as the other. So we still have a way to go" (p. 184).

This same sentiment is expressed in a recent article published in *Hispanic* (September 1999). In "A Passion for History: A Conversation With Rudolfo Anaya," Martha Espinoza interviews the author in the Westin Hotel in Chicago. Anaya expresses his ideas about Chicanos—their literary, political, and cultural heritage. He states, "You don't stop searching in your own community. From there you can go to other civilizations, other literatures, other histories and you begin to discover that, as human beings, we have a lot in common. The more you go back to understand origins of groups of people or civilizations, the more you understand yourself" (p. 65). Nothing is lost.

Chapter 9

Notes From the Writer's Journal

"Anaya, Godfather and Guru of Chicano Literature . . ."
Tony Hillerman

Writing this book can be compared to researching a term paper for English class. I followed the procedures that students do after they select a topic for their projects—gather information, take notes, write several rough drafts, proofread, revise, and submit the final copy. Teachers emphasize the need for both primary and secondary sources. My topic was fascinating from the beginning of the project to the end because I was writing the first biography of this talented man.

Young scholars should learn the process through which a book is created and published. They need to meet authors and communicate with them. Rudolfo Anaya receives many notes and letters from students as they study his works in Chicano Literature. He writes to them and sends autographed copies of his books for use in preparing their research papers and oral presentations. Also, he grants interviews to young people who are writing projects based on his works. His accessibility has made him a highly respected author throughout the Southwest.

It was two years ago that I approached Rudolfo Anaya in San Angelo, Texas, with my idea about writing his life story. We were both featured in a Southwestern/Chicano Literature Symposium honoring Elmer Kelton, and sponsored by the Angelo State University English Department. My publisher, Edwin Eakin, and his wife hosted a dinner party in a beautiful Mexican food restaurant called "Mejor Que Nada," owned by my friend Ray Zapata, former member of the Board of Regents that governs our university.

My talk preceded Anaya's, and I was introduced by Dr. James Hindman, president of Angelo State University, a friend and colleague since our days as young professors at Sul Ross State University and school board trustees of the Alpine ISD in the 1970s. As I stepped up to the podium, I saw Rudolfo Anaya sitting in the front row, wearing a sweater, jeans, and baseball cap. I went up to him, embraced him, and he whispered, "Take it easy and imagine that you are teaching your Chicano Literature class."

With that advice, I spoke about my approach to teaching *Bless Me, Ultima* before an audience of educators and writers. I had my copies of his novels, all autographed first editions, displayed on a table in front of me. During the year, I had compiled a scrapbook of articles, reviews, and pictures that were published about my book, *Keep Blessing Us, Ultima* (Eakin Press, 1997) and brought it along as well.

Rudolfo Anaya was next on the program. Dr. Gloria

Duarte Valverde, assistant professor of English, introduced him, and the audience gave him a standing ovation. He was in top form that night as he spoke before a standing-room-only audience. He had many messages to give to the audience. Anaya read representative passages from his books and peppered his talk with puns, anecdotes, *dichos,* and philosophical observations about the human condition. As I glanced around the room, I saw the intensity on people's faces as they listened to the Man of Aztlan.

After his talk, he autographed books and answered questions from the audience. We both signed books in the foyer. We talked about many things that night, especially my plans to teach the Rudolfo Anaya course at Sul Ross State University. He agreed to a teleconference with my students before the end of the term. We had time to listen to each other's papers and exchange ideas. He offered good advice to me about writing and publishing.

After a nice party hosted by Dr. Arnoldo DeLeon, professor of history at ASU, and his wife, Lupe, in honor of my colleague, Dr. Felipe de Ortego y Gasca, I retired to my room and reviewed my notes for the next day. Rudolfo Anaya would address the students the next morning. I wanted to hear the presentation and see their response.

The presentation for the students was received enthusiastically. Rudolfo looked rested and comfortable as he spoke about the importance of multicultural literature in contemporary society. Dr. Gloria Valverde's Chicano Literature students asked interesting questions and responded favorably to his comments and readings. After a short question and answer period, followed by an auto-graph session, Arnoldo, Lupe, Gloria, Felipe, and I accompanied Anaya to the airport for his flight back to Albuquerque. He liked the idea of the biography.

A week later, I began to write the book. Following the writing regimen described to me by my role models, Rudolfo Anaya, Richard Rodriguez, Mark Medoff, Edward Albee, Luis Valdez, Carlos Fuentes, and Denise Chavez, I set out to portray Anaya in an honest and sincere manner.

I discovered that I am a night writer. Richard Rodriguez tells me that I have a "night face," a creative mask, half shadow and half light, that a writer wears as he sits in the glow of the computer and composes. With intense concentration and isolation from the outside world, the writer finds the magic of the letters. I am interested in the writing schedule that my writer friends follow and their outlets for relaxation, and so I decided to find out.

Rudolfo Anaya

Rudolfo Anaya writes early in the morning until noon every day. In the afternoon, he takes a siesta to relax and reads voraciously—best sellers, newspapers, magazines, anthologies, biographies, and children's books. He answers correspondence, converses with his agent and publishers at Warner Books, and spends quality time with Patricia.

A man with many commitments in Albuquerque, Anaya makes appearances in the public schools and attends numerous civic and social functions. He told me that he gives talks and readings and attends symposiums all over the country. He travels as much as his schedule allows. In 1999 he and Patricia took a New Year's cruise to Spain, Portugal, and Morocco. Anaya says that he relaxes by taking long walks or spending time at Jemez Springs.

Carlos Fuentes

Carlos Fuentes also writes in the morning after having his coffee and reading the morning paper. He stops writing at noon and has lunch with his wife and children. In the afternoons, he may go for a stroll in Mexico City, and he reads everything possible—fiction, history, and biography. When I met him last winter in Georgetown, Texas, during the Brown Symposium (in which he and Guatemalan writer and Nobel Prize winner Rigoberta Menchu were featured speakers), he told me over breakfast that he likes to go to the symphony with his wife, either in Mexico City or in London.

Richard Rodriguez

Richard Rodriguez also writes in the morning and takes time in the afternoon to read, revise his projects, and answer correspondence. In a telephone conversation with him (October 20, 1999), he explained that he composes daily in his office in San Francisco. He works on a variety of projects and reads newspapers, magazines, reviews, and journals voraciously. To relax, he jogs, wrestles, and works out at Gold's Gym in San Francisco to relieve stress. He was completing his third book, *Brown,* lecturing all over the country, and fulfilling his obligations as associate editor for the Pacific News Service and contributing editor for the *Los Angeles Times*. I am grateful to Richard for his advice and guidance in matters related to writing and publishing.

Denise Chavez

During the annual Borderlands Folktale Festival at Sul Ross State University, Chicana fiction writer Denise Chavez of Las Cruces, New Mexico, told the audience that she writes at night after she relaxes and takes care of her household duties. She walks from her house to her studio and writes her novels and short stories in the glow of her scented candles. "There's something solitary and spiritual to walk back to my house from my studio at four o'clock in the morning when the world is about to wake up. I see the newspaper man making his rounds at this time of the morning," she says. I interviewed Denise two weeks before the festival for KSRC, Sul Ross State University's radio station, and the program was broadcast as part of the publicity for the program. She spoke of her plans to write a novel featuring legendary Mexican singer/actor Pedro Infante.

Night Face

Like Denise Chavez, I write at night when I can light candles and listen to classical music as part of the ambience. After years of taking care of my nurturing mother and my beloved sister, who are both with God, I have learned to be alone and appreciate my privacy. Most of all, I have developed my craft as a writer by practicing, reading constantly, and listening to the advice given by my mentors.

A conversation with Rudolfo Anaya gives me the motivation to write. He and I communicate through letters and telephone calls. When I ask for advice and information, he always takes time to talk to me and sends materials that I need for the project on which I am working. For example, when I completed the first half of this manuscript and mailed it to him, he called back and said, "Abelardo, I have some good news! Your manuscript is excellent! You have finally found your writing voice!"

From that point on, I plunged steadfast into the manuscript because I wanted the biography to present an authentic and realistic portrayal of the writer as artist.

The best opportunity came when I was given a chance to write a 2,500-word biographical essay for the *Dictionary of Literary Biography,* edited by Richard Cracroft, Ph.D., of Brigham Young University. After a year of researching, writing, and revising, I submitted the final copy to the *DLB.* The piece was published in May 1999, and I sent copies to Anaya and my publisher, Edwin Eakin. I wanted my publisher to examine the possibilities of developing the essay into a biography for young readers. Nothing had been lost.

Chapter 10

Man of Aztlan

"Amor y esperanza. And a new dream."
(Shaman Winter, p. 374)

On May 4, 1999, Rudolfo Anaya and I had an interesting telephone conversation. He told me the title of his forthcoming children's book, *My Land Sings: Tales from the Rio Grande* (Morrow Junior Books, 1999). When I heard the wonderful title, I experienced a catharsis that prompted me to write the last part of the book. I had a vision of *Man of Aztlan* in the same manner Anaya did when he saw the old woman as he struggled to write *Bless Me, Ultima.*

I visualized the book in my mind, from the cover to the chronology. Rudolfo had sent me a photo, and it would be perfect for the cover. It is a striking black and white picture of him in a black sweater, looking into the distance. He has the aura of a visionary. I envisioned pictures of him at various stages of his life. In my mind's eye, the book was written that night.

La Luz de los Farolitos

Two weeks later, I received an advance copy of *Farolitos for Abuelo* (Hyperion, 1999), a sequel to the famous *The Farolitos of Christmas* (1987). It has a message of life, death, hope, and resurrection. Luz's grandfather dies after saving a young boy who falls in a river. The chilling waters give Abuelo a terrible cold that develops into pneumonia. Abuelo dies, and Luz is seen kneeling next to the coffin in the *sala,* or parlor. The *luminarias* that welcome Luz's father from the war in the first book are seen around Abuelo's tombstone. Luz learns a valuable lesson about life and the inevitability of death. Abuelo's spirit lives in *la luz de los faroles.* She promises to light *farolitos* for Abuelo at Christmas and plant in his garden during the spring. Abuelo will always be with her.

Farolitos for Abuelo helps children understand the image of death. Those who read it will hear his voice. The plot is a symphony with many different sounds, from the rushing of the chilling waters to the sounds of silence felt by Luz as she kneels near Abuelo's coffin. The *farolitos* placed around his tombstone bring the music heard in *Farolitos of Christmas* as the carolers sing their songs of joy and peace. The illustrations by Edward Gonzales are vivid and realistic.

In reading Anaya's literature, young readers feel the magic of realism in his cultural arias. *La Llorona* has the tragic beauty of an opera like Puccini's *La Boheme. Llorona's* moments of insanity as she searches frantically for her offspring in *Maya's Children* remind readers of Lady Macbeth as she rubs and curses the imaginary spots of blood on her hands.

Billy the Kid is a *vaquero* with a price on his head, similar to Robin Hood in Sherwood Forest and Gregorio Cortez in South Texas. These outlaws are chased by lawmen on charges of theft and murder. They become heroes when they defend the plights of the poor. Their adventures are told in *corridos,* or ballads, that float in the winds of Aztlan.

When I read *A Chicano in China,* I can hear the chimes of oriental music emanating from the pages. When I teach *Matachines,* the music from Plaza Vieja sets the tone for the symbolic dance of the *Monarca* between Cristina and Andres dressed as Malinche and El Toro. My favorite is *The Farolitos of Christmas.* As Luz and Reina prepare for *la noche buena,* Christmas Eve, they hear the hymns of Navidad being sung by a group of madrigals outside. Their *cantos* are a universal celebration of the human spirit. As listeners, we are swept into a world of magic and peace.

Epiphany

As readers of Rudolfo Anaya's literature, we hear the music in the chanting of Ultima in the *llano,* wrapped in her shawl... in the heart of the city as Jason becomes a man... in Tortuga's blue guitar... in the dance of the *Monarca*... in the silence of the *llano*... *en la tierra amarilla*... in the *cuentos* of the Hispanic Southwest... in the wailing of Malinche as she is covered by darkness... in the ears of a Chicano in China... in the ballad of Billito... in Angie's rocking chair... in the mind of Sonny Baca... in the mystery of four black feathers... in the frightened cries of Maya... in the Calendar of Dreams... in the legend of Quetzalcoatl... and in the voice of Rudolfo Anaya. This is his song of Aztlan as we hear it.

Chronology

1937 | Born 30 October to Martin Anaya and Rafaelita Mares in Pastura, New Mexico. The family moves to Santa Rosa.

He is one of nine children—Larry, Martin, Edwina, Angelina, Rudolfo, Dolores, Loretta, Salomon, and Elvira.

1952 | The Anaya family moves to Albuquerque, New Mexico. Rudolfo attends Washington Junior High School.

1953 | Rudolfo Anaya is injured in a near-fatal diving accident and hospitalized.

1956 | Graduates from Albuquerque High School.

1956–58 | Attends Browning Business School.

1963 | Receives B.A. degree in English from the University of New Mexico.

1963–72 | Teaches English in Albuquerque public schools.

1966 | Marries Patricia Lawless of Kansas.

1968 | Receives M.A. degree in English from the University of New Mexico.

1972 | *Bless Me, Ultima* published by Quinto Sol Publications, Inc., Berkeley, California.

Receives Premio Quinto Sol Award for *Bless Me, Ultima*.

1972–74	Serves as director of counseling at the University of Albuquerque.
1974	Begins professorship in creative writing at University of New Mexico.
1976	*Heart of Aztlan* is published.
1979	*Tortuga* is published.
1980	Receives major awards—National Endowment for the Arts Fellowship; New Mexico Governor's Award for Excellence in Literature; Before Columbus American Book Award for *Tortuga*.
	Translates *Tales: Cuentos of the Hispanic Southwest* with Jose Griego y Maestas.
1981	Receives Honorary Doctorate of Humane Letters from the University of New Mexico.
1982	*Silence of the Llano* is published.
1982–86	Awarded three-year W.K. Kellogg Foundation National Fellowship.
1982	Co-edits *Cuentos Chicanos: A Short Story Anthology* with Antonio Marquez.
1984	*The Legend of La Llorona* is published.
	Receives Doctorate of Humane Letters from Marycrest College, Davenport, Iowa.
1985	*The Adventures of Juan Chicaspatas* (epic poem) is published.
1986	*A Chicano in China* (travel journal) is published.
1987	*Lord of the Dawn: The Legend of Quetzalcoatl* is published.
	The Farolitos of Christmas (children's picture book) is published.
	Edits *Voces: An Anthology of Nuevo Mexicano Writers.*
	Who Killed Don Jose? (play) is published.

1989	Edits *Tierra: Contemporary Short Fiction of New Mexico.*
	Co-edits *Aztlan: Essays on the Chicano Homeland.*
1992	World premiere of *Matachines* 10 December, Albuquerque, New Mexico.
1993	Retires from professorship at the University of New Mexico.
1994	*Bless Me, Ultima* is re-issued by Warner Books.
	Honorary Doctorate of Humane Letters from California Lutheran University.
1995	*Zia Summer* is published.
	The Anaya Reader is published.
	The Farolitos of Christmas (children's illustrated book) is published by Hyperion Press.
1996	*Rio Grande Fall* (novel) is published.
1997	*Maya's Children* (children's book) is published.
	Receives Honorary Doctorate of Humane Letters from the University of New Hampshire.
1999	*Shaman Winter* is published.
	Farolitos for Abuelo (children's book) is published by Hyperion Press.
	My Land Sings: Stories from the Río Grande (children's book) is published by Morrow Junior Books, New York.

Rudolfo Anaya
Career Vita

Personal:

Born October 30, 1937, Pastura, New Mexico.

Major Fields:

English and American Literature, Creative Writing.

Education:

M.A. Literature, 1968, University of New Mexico (UNM).

M.A. Guidance and Counseling, 1972, UNM.

B.A. Literature, 1963, UNM.

Browning Business School, 1956-58.

Albuquerque High School, graduated 1956.

Teaching Experience:

1999—Literary Sojourn, Steamboat Springs, Colorado.

1997—Guest professor, Feaver-MacMinn Seminar and Lecture, University of Oklahoma.

1997—Aspen Writers Conference keynote address.

1996—Martin Luther King, Jr./Cesar Chavez, Rosa Parks Visiting Professorship, University of Michigan, Ann Arbor.

1993—Retired from teaching. Professor Emeritus, UNM.

1974-1993—Professor, Dept. of Language and Literature, (English Department) UNM.

1971-1973—Director, Counseling Center, University of Albuquerque.

1974—Lecturer, Universidad Anahuac, Mexico City.

1963-1970—Teacher, Albuquerque Public Schools. Aspen Writers Conference, Squaw Valley Writers Conferences, Literary Sojourn, and many other writer conferences.

Honorary (Ph.D.) Doctor Degrees Awarded:

1997—Doctor of Humane Letters, University of New Hampshire.

1996—Doctor of Literature, *honoris causa,* University of New Mexico.

1994—Honorary Ph.D., Doctor of Humane Letters, California Luthern University, Thousand Oaks, CA.

1992—Honorary Ph.D., Doctor of Humane Letters, University of New England, Biddeford, Maine.

1991—Honorary Ph.D. College of Santa Fe, Santa Fe, NM.

1984—Honorary Ph.D., Doctor of Humane Letters, Marycrest College, Davenport, Iowa, May 1984.

1981—Honorary Ph.D., Doctor of Humane Letters, University of Albuquerque.

Publications:

Elegy of the Death of César Chávez, November 2000.

Roadrunner's Dance, November 2000.

Shaman Winter, novel, 1999 (Warner Books).

My Land Sings: Stories From the Rio Grande, 10 stories for young adults, 1999 (Wm. Morrow).

Farolitos for Abuelo, children's picture book, 1999 (Hyperion).

Isis in the Heart, 1998, Valley of Kings Press (special ed.).

Descansos: An Interrupted Journey, with Estevan Arellano and Denise Chavez (1997, Academia/El Norte Publications, NM).

Rio Grande Fall, novel (Warner Books, 1996).

Jalamanta, A Message From the Desert (Warner Books, 1996).

Maya's Children, children's picture book (Hyperion, 1997).

The Farolitos of Christmas, children's picture book (Hyperion, 1995).

Zia Summer, a novel (Warner Books, 1995).

The Anaya Reader, anthology of essays, stories, plays (Warner Books, 1995). Warner Books issued a hard cover edition, a mass market, and a Spanish edition of *Bless Me Ultima.* And issued *Alburquerque,* paperback, 1994.

Alburquerque, novel (UNM Press, Albuquerque, NM, 1992).

Tortuga, novel, Polish edition (Wydawnictwe Literackie Krakow, Poland, 1990).

Tierra, Contemporary Short Fiction of New Mexico, editor (Cinco Puntos Press, El Paso, Texas, 1989).

Aztlan, Essays on the Chicano Homeland, co-editor, Francisco Lomeli (El Norte Publications/Academia, Albuquerque, 1987).

Voces, An Anthology of Nuevo Mexicano Writers, editor (El Norte Publications/Academia, Albuquerque, 1987).

Lord of the Dawn/The Legend of Quetzalcoatl, novel (University of New Mexico Press, Albuquerque, 1987).

The Farolitos of Christmas, a children's Christmas story, *New Mexico Magazine,* Santa Fe, NM, 1987 (see Hyperion Edition).

A Chicano in China, travel journal (University of New Mexico Press, 1986).

The Adventures of Juan Chicaspatas, epic poem (Houston: Arte Publico Press, 1985).

The Legend of La Llorona, a short novel (Quinto Sol
Publications, Berkeley, CA, 1984).

Cuentos Chicanos—A Short Story Anthology, co-edited with
Antonio Marquez (University of New Mexico Press,
Albuquerque, NM, 1984).

The Silence of the Llano, short story collection (Quinto
Sol/Tonatiuh Publications, Berkeley, CA, 1982).

The Magic of Words, bilingual essay for UNM Library, ed. Paul
Vassalo, Dean, UNM Library (UNM Press, 1982).

Cuentos: Tales from the Hispanic Southwest, English translation
of Hispanic folktales (Museum of New Mexico Press, Santa
Fe, NM, 1980).

Tortuga, novel (Editorial Justa Publications, Berkeley, CA,
1979; University of New Mexico Press current edition).

Voices from the Rio Grande, co-editor (Rio Grande Writers
Association, 1976).

Heart of Aztlan, novel (Editorial Justa Publications, Berkeley,
CA, 1976; UNM Press current edition).

Bless Me, Ultima, novel (Quinto Sol Publications, Berkeley, CA,
1972). *Bless Me, Ultima* won the 1971 Premio Quinto Sol.
Tortuga won the 1976 American Book Award from Before
Columbus Foundation, and *Albuquerque* won the 1993
Fiction Award from PEN-WEST.

Autobiography:

Autobiography appears in *Contemporary Authors-Autobiography
Series* (Gale Research Co. Volume 4).

Interviews:

Interviews appear in *Conversations with Rudolfo Anaya,* Eds.
Bruce Dick and Silvio Sirias (University of Mississippi Press,
1999).

Translations:

Current translations of novels in Mexico, Russia, France, Germany, Italy, and Japan. Short stories and essays have been published in many literary magazines in USA and abroad. Excerpts from novels, short stories and essays in various textbooks, anthologies, and literary magazines.

Dramas:

Angie produced Summer 1998, Albuquerque, NM.

Billy the Kid produced Summer 1997, Albuquerque, NM.

Ay, Compadre produced, Su Teatro, Denver en La Casa, Albuquerque, NM, and San Diego, CA.

Death of a Writer

The Farolitos of Christmas, play produced by La Compania, Albuquerque, NM, December 1987, 1990, 1993, and 1995.

Who Killed Don Jose?, play in *New Mexico Plays,* edited by David Richard Jones, 1989 (UNM Press), produced 1987.

Matachines, a play. Produced by La Compania, Albuquerque.

The Season of La Llorona, a one-act play, produced 1979.

Editing:

Blue Mesa Review, founding editor, editor 1989-1993. Co-editor, *Voices From the Rio Grande,* Rio Grande Writers Association, 1976. Co-editor, *Ceremony of Brotherhood,* Academia Publications, Albuquerque, 1981. German edition of *Bless Me, Ultima,* published in 1984, Horst Tonn, translator, Nexus Verlag, Frankfurt. Spanish edition of *Bless Me, Ultima,* Editorial Grijalbo, 1993, Mexico City.

Honors and Awards:

2000—Tomás Rivera Mexican American Children's Book Award for *My Land Sings,* September 21, San Marcos, TX.

2000—Arizona Adult Author Award by Arizona Library Association, November 17.

2000—Albuquerque High School Millennium Celebration Outstanding Graduate Award (one of 300), August 5.

2000—De Colores Hispanic Leadership Award in Literature, September 16, Albuquerque.

1997—Distinguished Achievement Award, Western Literature Association, October 17, 1997, Albuquerque, NM.

1997—Premio Fronterizo awarded by Border Book Festival, Las Cruces, NM.

1995—Tomas Rivera, Mexican American Children's Book Award for *The Farolitos of Christmas.*

1995—Excellence in the Humanities Award, New Mexico Endowment for the Humanities.

El Fuego Nuevo Award, Association of Mexican American Educators, Los Angeles, CA.

Art Achievement Award, Hispanic Heritage Celebration, Albuquerque.

1994—Erna S. Fergusson Award conferred by University of New Mexico Alumni Association for exceptional accomplishments.

1993—PEN-WEST Award for Fiction, *Alburquerque* novel.

1991—Awarded a Rockefeller Foundation Residency, Bellagio, Italy.

PEN Center USA West, Freedom to Write Award.

Mesa College Humanities Award, Mesa College, San Diego, CA.

1990—In Appreciation, Chicana/Latina Literary Association Award, California State University, Sacramento, CA.

1990–93—Three-year University of New Mexico Regents' Professorship.

1990—UNM Regents' Meritorious Service Medal, English Department, Elizabeth H. Wertheim Lectureship.

1989—Awarded the UNM Annual Research Lectureship. New Mexico Eminent Scholar Award.

1986—Mexican Medal of Friendship awarded by the Mexican Consulate in Albuquerque, NM.

1983–86—Three-year W. K. Kellogg Foundation Fellowship Award, a fellowship for research, writing, and travel.

1983—Award for Achievement in Chicano Literature, Hispanic Caucus, NCTE, Denver, Colorado, November 19, 1983.

Certificate of Appreciation, Eastern New Mexico University, Reading Conference, June 3, 1983.

1982—UNM sabbatical, January through December 1982.

1981—Honorary member, Sigma Delta Pi, University of Albuquerque. Award for literature, Delta Kappa Gamma, New Mexico.

1980—Fellowship, National Endowment for the Arts (NEA), New Mexico Governor's Award for Excellence and Achievement in Literature.

Invited by Mrs. Carter and President Carter to read at the White House, "Salute to American Poets and Writers."

Outstanding Graduate Award, Albuquerque High School 100th Celebration.

1979—The Before Columbus American Book Award for *Tortuga*. Fellowship, National Chicano Council of Higher Education.

1978—New Mexico Governor's Public Service Award.

1977—Awards by City of Los Angeles.

UNM Mesa Chicana Literary Award.

1971—Premio Quinto Sol, national literary award, for *Bless Me, Ultima*.

Travel:

Mexico, Canada, Europe, China, South and Central America, Israel, Turkey, Greece, Egypt, Morocco.

Professional Activities:

Associate editor, *The American Book Review.*

Board of contributing editors, *The Americas Review.*

Advisory editor, *Great Plains Quarterly.*

Member, National Association of Chicano Studies.

Founder and first president, N.M. Rio Grande Writers Association.

Board member, Before Columbus Foundation.

1991, founder of RETE, now known as TECLA (Teachers of English and Chicano Language Arts).

1989–1998 Director and founder of the Kookooee projects.

Founder, PEN-NEW MEXICO, a PEN chapter.

International:

1996—France, St. Malo Book Fair.

1995—April, USIS sponsored lectures at six Italian universities. September, USIS lectures in Barcelona, Madrid. Leon, Spain Summer Institute, and University of Lisbon, Portugal.

1994—Lectures in Bordeaux, France, Heidelberg, Germany, and Guadalajara Book Fair.

1992 and 1994—Guadalajara Book Fair, Mexico.

1990—Book Fair in Nicaragua.

1988—Conference on Hispanics in the U.S., Barcelona, Spain. (June 1988, attended UNM Scholars Exchange Program with Trujillo, Spain.)

March 11–21, 1986—Paris, France, Conference on Hispanic and Chicano literature, lecture at the University of Bordeaux.

January 19–31, 1986—United States Information Agency sponsored lectures at American Studies Conference in Israel and the University in Haifa.

October 3–15, 1985—Final Kellogg Foundation Fellowship project trip to Switzerland. Attended Frankfurt Book Fair in Frankfurt.

November 8–22, 1984—Brazil International Seminar, traveled to Rio de Janeiro, Salvador, Forteleza, Belem, Manaus; field trips to rural clinics and hospitals, the Amazon River and the rain forest.

November 22–29, 1984—Kellogg Fellowship, travel to Peru included visits to Lima, Cuzco, and Macchu Picchu.

May 12 – June 13, 1984—Kellogg Fellowship, tour of China; travel to Beijing, Xian, Chongguing, Chengdu, Shanghai, and Hangzhou.

October 23–25, 1983—Interaccion Cultural Fronteriza, at the III PROFMEX-ANUIES Bilateral Symposium of the Universities of Mexico and the United States, at Tijuana, Mexico.

1982—Quebec Writers Exchange, Trois Rivieras, Quebec.

1982—Delegate, "Dialogo de las Americas," International Conference of the Sovereignty of the American Nations, Mexico City, Mexico.

Works Consulted

BOOKS BY RUDOLFO ANAYA:

Bless Me, Ultima (Berkeley, CA: Quinto Sol, 1972).

Heart of Aztlan (Berkeley, CA: Editorial Justa, 1976).

Tortuga (Berkeley, CA: Editorial Justa, 1979).

Cuentos Chicanos: A Short Story Anthology by Rudolfo Anaya and Antonio Marquez (Albuquerque: University of New Mexico Press, 1984).

Cuentos: Tales from the Hispanic Southwest by Rudolfo Anaya and Jose Griego y Maestas (Santa Fe, New Mexico: Museum of New Mexico Press, 1980).

The Silence of the Llano: Short Stories (Berkeley, CA: Tonatiuh-Quinto Sol, 1982).

The Legend of La Llorona (Berkeley, CA: Tonatiuh-Quinto Sol, 1984).

The Adventures of Juan Chicaspatas (Houston: Arte Publico, 1985).

A Chicano in China (Albuquerque: University of New Mexico Press, 1986).

The Farolitos of Christmas, illustrations by Edward Gonzales (New York: Hyperion Books for Children, 1995).

Lord of the Dawn: The Legend of Quetazalcoatl (Albuquerque: University of New Mexico Press, 1987).

The Anaya Reader (New York: Warner Books, 1995).

Zia Summer (New York: Warner Books, 1995).

Jalamanta: A Message from the Desert (New York: Warner Books, 1996).

Rio Grande Fall (New York: Warner Books, 1996).

Maya's Children: The Story of La Llorona, illustrations by Maria Baca (New York: Hyperion Books for Children, 1997).

Farolitos for Abuelo, illustrations by Edward Gonzales (New York: Hyperion Books for Children, 1999).

Shaman Winter (New York: Warner Books, 1999).

AUTOBIOGRAPHY:

"Rudolfo A. Anaya: An Autobiography." *Contemporary Authors: Autobiography Series,* Volume 4, edited by Adele Sarkissan. Gale Research Company, 1986.

ESSAY:

Shaman of Words, essay, Genre (University of Oklahoma, 1999).

PLAYS:

The Season of La Llorona, La Compania de Teatro, Albuquerque, 14 October 1987.

Who Killed Don Jose? Albuquerque, La Compania Menaul High School Theatre, July 1987.

The Farolitos of Christmas, Albuquerque, La Compania de Teatro, Menaul High School Theatre, December 1987.

Matachines, Albuquerque, La Compania de Teatro, 10 December 1992.

Ay, Compadre, Albuquerque, Su Casa Teatro, 1987.

Billy the Kid, Albuquerque, Su Casa Teatro, 11 July 1997.

Angie, Albuquerque, Su Casa Teatro, 10 July 1998.

REFERENCES:

Abelardo Baeza, "Chiconics: The Voice of the Barrio," *Journal of Big Bend Studies* (Volume IX, 1997), 157-163.

Bruce Dick and Silvio Sirias, eds. *Conversations with Rudolfo Anaya* (Jackson: University of Mississippi Press, 1998).

Martha Espinoza, "A Passion for History: A Conversation with Rudolfo Anaya," *Hispanic* (September 1999) 64–65.

Juan Bruce-Novoa, "Rudolfo A. Anaya," in his *Chicano Authors: Inquiry by Interview* (London and Austin: University of Texas Press, 1989), pp. 183-202.

Phillip D. Ortego, ed., *We Are Chicanos: An Anthology of Mexican-American Literature* (New York: Washington Square Press, 1973).

Antonia Castaneda Shular, Tomas Ybarra-Frausto, Joseph Sommers, eds., *Literatura Chicana: Texto y Contexto* (Englewood Cliffs, New Jersey: Prentice-Hall, Inc., 1972).

César A. González-T. and Phyllis S. Morgan, *A Sense of Place: Rudolfo A. Anaya: An Annotated Bio-Bibliography* (Berkeley, CA: University of California, Ethnic Studies Library Publications Unit), 2000.